Language Variation in South Asia

Language Variation in South Asia

WILLIAM BRIGHT

New York Oxford
OXFORD UNIVERSITY PRESS
1990

Oxford University Press

Oxford New York Toronto
Delhi Bombay Calcutta Madras Karachi
Petaling Jaya Singapore Hong Kong Tokyo
Nairobi Dar es Salaam Cape Town
Melbourne Auckland

and associated companies in
Berlin Ibadan

Published by Oxford University Press, Inc.,
200 Madison Avenue, New York, NY 10016

Library of Congress Cataloging-in-Publication Data
Bright, William, 1928–
Language variation in South Asia / by William Bright.
p. cm. Includes bibliographical references.
ISBN 0-19-506365-1
1. Dravidian languages—Variation.
2. South Asia—Languages—Variation.
3. Diglossia (Linguistics) I. Title.
PL4603.B7 1990 494'.8—dc20
90-31688

2 4 6 8 9 7 5 3 1

Printed in the United States of America
on acid-free paper

प्रियायै मे सहचारिण्यै सप्रेम समर्पितम्

Lise Menn

Preface

My introduction to South Asian linguistics, as a student at Berkeley, was through the teaching of M. B. Emeneau; starting in 1948, he gave me my start in Sanskrit and in comparative Dravidian. At the same time, with the added guidance of Mary R. Haas, I was beginning work on American Indian linguistics; it was in this latter field that my doctorate was awarded in 1955. But jobs in linguistics were scarce then, and with Emeneau's support, I accepted a two-year Rockefeller Foundation fellowship to go to India. My duties there were to teach linguistics courses at Deccan College, Poona, during two short sessions each year, but otherwise to live in Mysore State (now Karnataka), working on a descriptive grammar of Kannada. Since only the literary variety of the language had been previously described, in the grammar of Spencer (1950), my specific purpose was to prepare an account of the colloquial language.

At that time I had little appreciation of the linguistic complexity of South Asia. While still in Berkeley, I had tried to prepare myself by recording spoken Kannada data from a graduate student of political science, a native of Mysore City. In the hope of eliciting data from the vernacular language, I asked him to speak to me as he would 'to a younger brother', and was only mildly surprised to find that his language was almost identical with that described by Spencer. In my innocence, I proceeded to Bangalore, the capital of Mysore State, and rented a house in the Cantonment area—only to find that my neighbors were quite ignorant of Kannada: their families had followed the British army from Madras State during the 19th century, and they spoke Tamil. Eventually my bicycle took me to the Kannada-speaking area of Bangalore, where I enlisted college students to help me learn the language. But my problems had not ended: the students taught me utterances like those I had read in Spencer, and had heard from my political scientist friend in Berkeley, but what I heard spoken on the street seemed a different language—no more intelligible to me than the Tamil of the Cantonment.

Eventually I discovered the solution to my problem. My consultants had been students of the humanities, educated in the belief that literary Kannada was the REAL language, to the point where they were convinced that it represented their everyday speech. But when I tried working with students of physical sciences and engineering, they proved able to give me EITHER literary or colloquial Kannada on request. They were indeed two different languages, at least on the phonological level. I had "discovered" diglossia—though I did not properly understand the phenomenon until, a few years later, I read the classic article on the subject by Charles Ferguson (1959). I once tried to prove to a 'literary' speaker that he really did use two languages: he swore that the only way to say "he doesn't do it" was *māḍuvudilla,* but I was able to confront him with a tape-recording of his own voice saying *māḍolla* to a family member. My victory was hollow, since the man stopped speaking to me.

On my periodic visits to Poona, I discovered that other linguists were having similar experiences; it was there I met Charles Ferguson and John Gumperz, who a few years later were to edit the first collection of papers on language variation in South Asia (1960). A new area of socially oriented linguistics seemed to be in the making. After returning to the United States in 1958, I became aware that William Labov was working on similar lines in regional varieties of American English (1963, 1964). Conferences on the emerging topic of SOCIOLINGUISTICS were held in 1963 and 1964 (published as Gumperz and Hymes 1964, Bright 1966c), and the field grew steadily from that time onward. By now, it has expanded to the point where few scholars can any longer claim expertise in the entire field.

After returning to the United States in 1957, I spent a year supervising classes in Hindi and Urdu at the State Department language school in Washington, D.C. After an interim year at Berkeley, I moved to Los Angeles in 1959, and from then onward worked at UCLA in the Department of Anthropology and (from 1966) the Department of Linguistics. There I found myself on a campus which had no organized program in South Asian studies, and only limited library facilities for the area. For that reason, Indological research took second place to my work on American Indian linguistics. Nevertheless, I was able to revisit India in 1967 and 1980, and to work at UCLA over the years with several students who were native speakers of Indian languages.

The chapters of the present volume have been adapted from articles published in various periodicals and collections between 1960 and 1988. They are presented here in chronological order, partially reflecting directions in which my linguistic interests have shifted over the years.

'Linguistic change in some Indian caste dialects' (1960) was my first paper in South Asian sociolinguistics, reporting the historical changes from literary Kannada revealed by two caste dialects of the spoken language—one used by Brahmins, one by non-Brahmins. 'Sociolinguistic variation and language change' (with A. K. Ramanujan 1964), examines comparable changes in Tamil and Tulu, and considers the role of literacy in the historical differentiation of social dialects. 'Dravidian metaphony' (1966) surveys a type of vowel assimilation widely attested in regional and social dialects of South India and Sri Lanka; attention is also drawn to parallel developments in non-Dravidian languages of South Asia, pointing to areal diffusion of the type established by Emeneau 1956, 1980. It may be noted that the evidence for the diffusion of grammatical structure between Dravidian and Indo-Aryan (in both directions) led me to reconsider the possible importance of such a process in historical relationships among the language families of North and South America. My work suggested the following:

(1) For language history in general, structural borrowing can be associated with an 'accommodative' mode of culture contact, attested throughout the history of South Asia, whereas constraints on linguistic borrowing are likely to be associated with a more 'separatist' mode of contact.

(2) Many researchers in comparative linguistics, especially with regard to Native America, have overemphasized 'family tree' relationships, to the neglect of areal ties.

(3) 'Language mixture' must be recognized as a factor of potential importance in studying the linguistic prehistory of any part of the world (Bright 1976, 1984).

Similar views have recently become increasingly accepted in the field of historical linguistics (see Thomason and Kaufman 1988).

'Language, social stratification, and cognitive orientation' (1966) examines differences in lexical semantics between caste dialects of several Dravidian languages, and suggests that the 'semantic isoglosses' which separate social groups within a larger speech community may correspond to psychological differences between such groups.

'Complex verb forms in colloquial Tamil' (with J. Lindenfeld 1968) is a descriptive study, using concepts from generative grammar, of the verb complex in an Ayyangar dialect of spoken Tamil. In retrospect, however, I must admit that what fascinated me most about the material was the historical development which it illustrated with respect to the conservative structure of written Tamil. Through processes of phonological and analogical change, combinations of tense suffixes and auxiliary verbs—conveying reflexivity, completed action, progressive action, and perfective action—have been reduced to minimal suffix-like elements, and long periphrastic sequences have turned into 'polysynthetic' words; e.g.,

/kuḑuX	-d-kk	-d-ūḑ	-d-kk + d-iruX	-d-iruX	-ar	-ā/
give	PAST-take (REFLEXIVE)	PAST-leave (COMPLETIVE)	PAST-take + PAST-be (PROGRESSIVE)	PAST-be (PERFECTIVE)	PRES	3SG.MASC

⇒ *kuḑuttunūṭṭirundirukkā* 'he has been giving it away for himself'

'Phonological rules in literary and colloquial Kannada' (1970) looks at data from the conservative written variety of Kannada and from the spoken dialects of several geographical and social communities, to consider the extent to which the relationships among them can be formulated in terms of ordered generative rules.

'Hindi numerals' (1972), the only paper here concerned exclusively with Indo-Aryan linguistics, focuses on individual variation in the complex morphological system of the numerals from 1 to 99, and sees this variation as the result of competition among alternative systems of intuitive rules. 'The Dravidian enunciative vowel' (1975) reviews the synchronic facts concerning a widespread pattern whereby an automatic vowel [ï] or [u] is added to stems and words with underlying final consonants—with many variations associated with social and geographical dialects—and attempts to explain these data in terms of historical and areal developments.

The last three papers are concerned with three questions regarding the relationship between the written and spoken variants of language (a topic of much recent interest, cf. Tannen 1982b), and the history of written language in ancient South Asia. 'How not to decipher the Indus Valley inscriptions' (1982) deals with the mysterious script used by the civilization of Harappa and Mohenjo-Daro in the 3rd millennium BCE, with the methodology appropriate for deciphering it—and with the conflicting claims that its linguistic links are to Sanskrit, on the one hand, or to Dravidian, on the other. 'Archaeology, linguistics, and Ancient Dravidian' (1986) is a critique of some attempts to bring archaeological data to bear on the problem of the Indus Valley script. Finally, 'Written and spoken language in South Asia' (1988) focuses on the puzzling fact that, after the decline of the Indus Valley civilization, we have no clear record of written language from South Asia for some 2,000 years (including the period when classical Sanskritic civilization reached its zenith) until the full-blown appearance of the Buddhist inscriptions of the Emperor Aśoka in the 3rd century BCE. It is argued here that written language must have existed in ancient India during the pre-Aśokan period, but that it played a very different social role than has been assumed by many modern scholars.

My greatest gratitude for help and inspiration in South Asian studies goes to M. B. Emeneau; his work has always been a major source of knowledge, an inspiration in the development of a sociolinguistic approach, and a model of what scholarship should be. In addition, I want to acknowledge my particular indebtedness to some of the South Asian scholars who have shared their knowledge and friendship with me: T. N. Sreekantaiya, P. B. Pandit, Bh. Krishnamurti, A. K. Ramanujan, and M. V. Nadkarni.

Boulder, Colorado W. B.
May 1990

Acknowledgments

The following chapters appearing in this volume are based on previous publications as listed below. Permission to reprint has been granted by coauthors and by publishers of the original articles, and is gratefully acknowledged.

Linguistic change in some Indian caste dialects. In *Linguistic diversity in South Asia,* ed. Charles A. Ferguson and John J. Gumperz, 19–26. Bloomington: Indiana University Research Center in Anthropology, Folklore and Linguistics, 1960.

Sociolinguistic variation and language change (with A. K. Ramanujan). *Proceedings of the Ninth International Congress of Linguists* (Cambridge, Mass., 1962), ed. Horace Lunt, 1107–13. The Hague: Mouton, 1964.

Dravidian metaphony. *Language* 43:311–22 (1966).

Language, social stratification, and cognitive orientation. In *Explorations in sociolinguistics,* ed. Stanley Lieberson *(Sociological Inquiry* 36:2), 313–18 (1966).

Complex verb forms in colloquial Tamil (with J. Lindenfeld). In *Studies in Indian linguistics (Prof. M. B. Emeneau Ṣaṣṭipūrti volume),* ed. Bh. Krishnamurti, 30–45. Poona: Linguistic Society of India, 1968.

Phonological rules in literary and colloquial Kanada. *Journal of the American Oriental Society* 90:140–44 (1970).

Hindi numerals. In *Studies in linguistics in honor of George L. Trager,* ed. M. Estellie Smith (Janua linguarum, series maior, no. 52), 222–30. The Hague: Mouton, 1972.

The Dravidian enunciative vowel. In *Dravidian phonological systems,* ed. Harold F. Schiffman and Carol M. Eastman, 11–46. Seattle: South Asian Studies Program, Institute for Comparative and Foreign Area Studies, University of Washington, 1975.

How not to decipher the Indus Valley inscriptions. Adapted from a review of *Studies in the Indus Valley inscriptions,* by J. E.

Mitchiner (1981). *Journal of the American Oriental Society* 102:233–35 (1982).

Archaeology, linguistics, and Ancient Dravidian. In *South Asian languages: Structure, convergence and diglossia,* ed. Bh. Krishnamurti, 108–12. Delhi: Motilal Banarsidass, 1986.

Written and spoken language in South Asia. In *On language: Rhetorica, Phonologica, Syntactica. A Festschrift for Robert P. Stockwell,* ed. Caroline Duncan-Rose and Theo Vennemann, 22–38. London: Routledge, 1988.

Contents

Language Variation in South Asia

1

Linguistic Change in Some Indian Caste Dialects

Dialect differences in the languages of India may be thought of in a three-dimensional framework: in addition to the horizontal distribution of geographical dialects, as is found throughout the world, India offers exceptionally clear cases of dialects which are spoken in a single spot, but which may be arranged in a vertical scale correlated with social class. These are the caste dialects, such as those of a North Indian village which have been described by Gumperz (1958). In the study of such dialects, the following question may be raised: Is there a correlation between the amount of linguistic change manifested in a dialect and the social status of the people who speak it? In other terms, in what caste dialects are the more archaic features to be found? Investigation of this question may require separate consideration of various parts of the language: that is, phonemic change, grammatical change, and lexical change may not all operate at the same speed in a given dialect.

This paper does not attempt to answer the question completely, but merely to contribute toward an answer, primarily by comparing data recorded from two Kannada dialects of Bangalore District, Mysore State, South India. One is a Brahmin dialect, as spoken by a young woman born and raised in the city of Bangalore. The other is of the agricultural Okkaliga community, as spoken by a young man from a village a few miles outside the city. Both informants have college educations.[1] The transcriptions are in terms of the following phonemes: /p t ṭ c k b d ḍ j g f s š z m n ṇ ŋ v l ḷ y r h i ī e ē ǣ ɨ a ā u ū o ō ɔ̄/ (see Bright 1958a). No attempt is made here to describe all existing differences between the two dialects in question; the differences which are described are those best attested in the data.

1. Phonological Differences

The phonemic systems of the two dialects display the following differences:

(1) The Brahmin dialect (hereafter abbreviated as B.) has the phonemes /f z ɔ̄/ in loanwords from English; in the Okkaliga dialect (O.) these are replaced by /p j ā/ respectively. E.g.: B. *kɔ̄fi,* O. *kāpi* 'coffee'; B. *ḍazan,* O. *ḍajan* 'dozen.'

(2) B. /c/, when intervocalic, sometimes corresponds to O. /s/: B. *samācāra,* O. *samāsāra* 'news', from Skt. *samācāra-*. The other cases noted are also loanwords. The data suggest that O. lacks contrast between /c/ and /s/, at least in medial position. This is reminiscent of the situation in Tamil, where affricate and fricative are members of one phoneme (Fowler 1954); the situation was probably the same in Primitive Dravidian.[2]

(3) B. /š/, occurring mainly in loanwords from Sanskrit, often corresponds to O. /s/: B. *šānti,* O. *sānti* 'peace'; B. *dēša,* O. *dēsa* 'country'; B. *kašṭa,* O. *kasṭa* 'difficulty'. (The B. forms are identical with the Sanskrit stems in each case.) The lack of contrast between /s/ and /š/ is also a characteristic of Tamil, and presumably of Primitive Dravidian.

(4) B. /h/ usually corresponds to O. zero: B. *hāku,* O. *āku* 'put'. After pause, B. /he hē ho hō/ correspond to O. /ye yē va vō/ respectively. This is in conformity with morphophonemic changes also operative in B., by which onglides are added to mid vowels after pause, and /vo/ is further replaced by /va/. E.g.: B. *hesru,* O. *yesru* 'name'; B. *hoge,* O. *vage* 'smoke'; B. *hōgu,* O. *vōgu* 'go'. In all these cases, the B. forms represent the earlier stage of development, reflecting PDr. forms with initial **p*: cf. OKa. *pesar,* Ta. *peyar,* Te. *pēru* 'name'; OKa. *poge,* Ta. *pukai,* Te. *poge* 'smoke'; OKa. *pōgu,* Ta. *pōku,* Te. *pōvu* 'go'.

(5) Aspirated stops of B. correspond to unaspirated ones in O. The examples are principally loanwords: B. *bhūmi,* O. *būmi* 'land' (Skt. *bhūmi-*).

(6) Syllable-initial consonant clusters, occurring in loanwords in B., are rare in O. Thus sequences of sibilant plus oral sonorant in B. correspond to /s/ alone in O.: B. *svāmi,* O. *sāmi* 'sir' (Skt. *svāmin-*); B. *manšya,* O. *mansa* 'man' (Skt. *manušya-*). B. /s/ plus nasal sometimes corresonds to O. /si/ plus nasal: B. *snēyta,* O. *sinēyta* 'friend' (Skt. *snehita-*). B. /kš/ corresponds to O. /c/: B. *kšemsu,* O. *cemsu* 'excuse me' (from Skt. √*kšam* 'to pardon'.)

(7) B. /ē/ often corresponds to O. /yā/ when a mid or low vowel occurs in the next syllable: B. *pēṭe,* O. *pyāṭe* 'town'. In these cases the pronunciation with /ē/ is older: cf. Ta. *pēṭṭai,* Marathi *peṭh.*

(8) B. /o/ often corresponds to O. /a/, as in the second morpheme of B. *mal-koḷḷ-ōṇa,* O. *mal-kaḷ-ani* 'let's go to bed'. This element, having reflexive meaning in Ka., is cognate with Ta. *koḷ* 'receive', Te. *konu* 'take'. Cf. also B. *barokke,* O. *barakke* 'for coming'; B. *āgolla,* O. *āgalla* 'doesn't become'. Both of these are contracted from forms such as the literary equivalents *bar-uvu-da-kke* and *āg-uvu-d-illa* respectively.

(9) B. /ɨ/ in the sequence /rɨ/, occurring in loans from Sanskrit, usually corresponds to O. /u/: B. *srɨŋgāra,* O. *suŋgāra* 'beauty' (Skt. *śṛŋgāra-*.)

The foregoing correspondences may be summarized as follows: Insofar as it fails to accept new phonemic contrasts occurring in loanwords, the O. dialect is the more archaic of the two. It is innovating, however, in its loss of earlier /h/, and in the changes of /ē/ to /yā/ and /o/ to /a/.

2. Grammatical Differences

The grammatical differences between the two dialects include the following:

(1) The dative suffix of B. has the allomorphs *-kke* after /a/ and *-Age* elsewhere. (*A* is a morphophoneme commonly actualized as zero after consonants; a vowel plus *A,* however, becomes immune to the syncope which otherwise affects short vowels.) This corresponds to O. *-ke* after nouns of all types: B. *ūṭa-kke,* O. *ūṭ-ke* (with syncope)

'to dinner'; B. *madve-ge,* O. *maduv-ke* 'to a wedding'; B. *mārkeṭ-ge,* O. *mārkeṭ-ke* 'to the market'. O. also has the variant *-kya:* B. *pēṭe-ge,* O. *pyāṭ-kya* 'to town'. Historically, B. *-kke* and *-Age* may be traced to OKa. *-kke* and *-ige* respectively. OKa. also has the form *-ke,* however (Narasimhia 1941:141–46); this has been lost in B., but generalized in O. to the point of replacing other allomorphs.

(2) Locative formations in B. contain an element *-alli,* corresponding to O. *-āgi*: B. *baṇḍy-alli* (also contracted to *baṇḍīli*), O. *baṇḍy-āgi* 'in a cart'. The B. form may be identified with the adverb *alli* 'there'; the O. form is of uncertain origin, though homonymous with *āgi* 'having become', from *āgu* 'become'. Formations in *-a!li* are attested in OKa., along with several other types lacking in the modern dialects (Narasimhia, 151–54); those in *-āgi* are apparently innovations.

(3) The first person plural imperative suffix is B. *-ōṇa,* O. *-āni, -ani, -ana.* E.g.: B. *hōg-ōṇa,* O. *vōg-āni* 'let's go'; B. *mugs-ōṇa,* O. *mugs-ani* 'let's finish'; B. *kūt-koḷḷ-ōṇa,* O. *kūt-koḷḷ-āna* 'let's sit down'. Cf. OKa. *-uvaṃ,* MKa. *-uva,* modern written Ka. *-uva, -uvana, -uvaṇa, -ōṇa.*[3] If, as is claimed by Kittel, /n/ is earlier than /ṇ/ in this suffix, then the O. forms are archaic in retaining it. The vowels of the O. forms, however, appear to be innovations.

(4) Certain verb stems show different allomorphy in the two dialects: *āgu* 'become', but B. *āg-ta,* O. *ā-ta* 'becoming'; B. *hōgu,* O. *vōgu* 'go', but B. *hōg-ta,* O. *vō-ta* 'going'; *bā* 'come', but B. *bar-ta,* O. *bat-ta* 'coming'. The O. forms are unattested in older Kannada. A different case, however, is B. *kū-tu,* O. *kun-tu* 'having sat' (from a stem occurring only in these forms); both of these date from the medieval period, being attested from 1398 and 1585 respectively (Kittel 1894:441, 457).

(5) The verb *iru* 'be' has a set of forms in B. which lack a tense suffix; corresponding to the third person forms of these, O. uses pronouns plus the emphatic morph *-e.* E.g.: B. *iddāne,* O. *avn-e* 'he is' (*avnu* 'he'); B. *iddāre,* O. *avr-e* 'they are' (*avru* 'they'); B. *ide,* O. *ad-e* 'it is' (*adu* 'it'). All of these are modern formations: of the O. forms, however, only the neuter *ad-e* is found in the modern written language (Kittel 1903:133–34). The other O. forms may represent an analogical extension on this model.

The foregoing grammatical correspondence thus show the B. dialect to be generally more archaic.

3. Lexical Differences

Finally, the following cases typify the differences of vocabulary between the two dialects (OKa. and other Dravidian forms are from Kittel's dictionary):

(1) In some cases, where there is only a slight phonemic difference between B. and O. forms, the B. form is known to be the earlier one. E.g.:

B. *horḍu,* O. *volḍu* 'start out'; cf. OKa. *poṟa, peṟa* 'out', Ta. *piṟ* 'outer', Malayalam *puṟ* 'outside', Te. *peṟ* 'foreign'.

B. *bāglu,* O. *bāklu* 'door'; cf. OKa. *bāgil.*

B. *bombe,* O. *gombe* 'doll'; cf. OKa. *bombe,* Ta. *pommai,* Te. *bomme.*

B. *matte,* O. *mante* 'again'; cf. OKa. *matte,* Ta. *maṟṟai.*

(2) In other cases, the O. form is known to be earlier; there is not necessarily any similarity between the two forms. E.g.:

B. *prayāṇa,* O. *payṇa* 'journey'. The B. form is a recent copy of Skt.; the O. forms is from OKa. *payaṇa,* which in turn is from Skt. *prayāṇa-* or *prayaṇa-*.

B. *bahḷa,* O. *balu* 'much, very'. Cf. MKa. *bahaḷa,* from Skt. *bahala;* but OKa. *bal* 'strength, greatness', Ta. *val,* Te. *balu.*

B. *togo,* O. *teko* 'take'; cf. OKa. *tekkoḷḷ-*.

B. *hēge,* O. *yeŋge* 'how'; cf. MKa. *hēge,* but OKa. *heŋge.*

B. *huḷi,* O. *yesru* 'curry'; cf. OKa. *esar.*

B. *ūṭa māḍu,* O. *uṇṇu* 'eat a meal'; cf. OKa. *uṇ,* Ta. *uṇ.*

(3) In the remaining cases, the relative age of the forms is not clear. E.g.:

B. *sumne,* O. *sumke* 'quiet'; cf. OKa. *summane* and *summage,* both attested in the same work.

B. *yešṭu,* O. *yēsu* 'how much', both attested in the same MKa. work.

B. *sarti,* O. *sāri* 'time, turn'. Both are attested only in modern times. The B. form may be from Skt. *sarat* 'going'; with the O. form, cf. Malayalam *sāri.*

B. *solpa,* O. *rav-asṭu* 'a little', both modern. The B. form is from Skt. *svalpa;* the O. form is literally 'as much as *(asṭu)* a grain *(rave)*', cf. Te. *rav-aste.*

B. *snāna māḍu,* O. *nīr āk-kō* 'bathe', both modern. B. is literally 'to make a bath', with Skt. *snāna-* 'bath'; O. is literally 'to put water on oneself':

B. *sinima,* O. *bayskōpu* 'movies', from English CINEMA and BIOSCOPE respectively; the former may be the more recent borrowing.

4. Conclusions

Generalizing from the above comparisons, we may draw the following conclusions: O. accepts foreign words and foreign phonemic patterns less readily than does B. Its vocabulary is thus more archaic, and its phonemic system is likewise archaic in that it lacks certain contrasts which B. has taken over from Sanskrit and other languages. B., on the other hand, is more resistant to phonemic changes of native sounds, and to grammatical change.

Reasons for B.'s receptiveness to importations from other languages are not hard to find: the Brahmins have traditionally been conversant with Sanskrit, and more recently with English. The prestige attached to both these languages has increased the likelihood for bilingual speakers to introduce words from them into Kannada. It is not quite as easy to account for the conservative tendency of B. as regards phonemic and grammatical change. A conditioning factor may be the greater literacy of the Brahmin community; that is, the permanence of the written word may retard change in the spoken language.

In this connection, data from Tulu, another Dravidian language of South India, deserves examination. Although separate dialects of Tulu are spoken by Brahmins and by non-Brahmins or Shudras, neither dialect is commonly written. We may therefore hypothesize that the B. dialect of Tulu wil show no greater retardation of phonetic change than the S. (Shudra) dialect. The Tulu data available shows, first of all, some correspondences in which the B. forms are more archaic:[4]

B. initial vowel corresponds to S. zero in a number of cases where PDr. has the initial vowel: B. *imboḷu,* S. *mōḷu* 'this woman' (Ta. *ivaḷ,* Ka. *ivaḷu*); B. *eḍaŋgɯ,* S. *ḍangɯ* 'left (hand)' (Ta. *iṭai,* Ka. *yeḍa*); B. *uṇpu,* S. *nuppu* 'food' (cf. Ta. *uṇ,* Ka. *uṇṇu* 'to eat'.)

B. /s/ corresponds to S. /t/ in some cases where PDr. has **c:* B. *sik-,* S. *tik-* 'be obtained' (Ta. *cikku,* Ka. *sikku*); in retaining sibilant quality, B. here appears more archaic.

B. /j/ corresponds to S. /d/ where PDr. has **ñ* (Burrow 1946:605) in B. *jeñji*, S. *deñji* 'crab' (Ta. *ñaṇṭu, ñeṇṭu,* Ka. *yēḍi*). B. appears more archaic, in that it retains palatal quality.

There are, however, other correspondences in which S. has the more archaic forms:

B. initial /ē/ corresponds to S. /yā/ in some cases where PDr. has **iā* (Burrow 1946:599): B. *ēnɯ*, S. *yānɯ* 'I' (Ta. *yāṉ*, OKa. *ān*); B. *ērɯ*, S. *yārɯ* 'who' (Ta. *yār, ār,* Ka. *yāru.*)

B. /s/ corresponds to S. /t/, where PDr. has **t*, in B. *sōj-*, S. *tōj-* 'appear' (Ta. *tōṉṟu*, Ka. *tōru.*)[5]

In another correspondence, both dialects innovate, and neither can be considered the more archaic. B. /ḷ/ corresponds to S. /r/ where PDr. has **ṟ̤*:[6] B. *bāḷæ*, S. *bāræ* 'plantain' (Ta. *vāṟ̤ai*, OKa. *bāṟ̤e*, modern *bāle*); B. *kōḷi*, S. *kōri* 'hen' (Ta. *koṟ̤i*, OKa. *kori*, modern *kōḷi*); B. *būḷ-*, S. *būr-* 'fall' (Ta. *viṟ̤-*, OKa. *būṟ̤-*, modern *bīḷu.*)

On the basis of the limited data, we may therefore conclude that the difference between B. and S. dialects of Tulu, as regards rate of phonetic change, is less marked than that between the B. and O. dialects of Kannaḍa. A further study of Tulu should be especially rewarding in the investigation of Indian caste dialects.

NOTES

1. The Brahmin idiolect presented here is that of my chief informant in an intensive study of the Bangalore Brahmin speech, and may be taken as typical. The Okkaliga dialect, on the other hand, was studied only briefly. The data obtained is not 'pure' Okkaliga speech; that is, the informant's idiolect has been influenced by the prestige of the Brahmin dialect. Even so, the salient features of Okkaliga speech show up clearly enough in the data recorded from him.

2. See Burrow (1947). Primitive Dravidian is hereafter abbreviated PDr.; so also Ka. for Kannada, OKa. for Old Kannada, MKa. for Medieval Kannada, Ta. for Tamil, Te. for Telugu, Skt. for Sanskrit.

3. See Kittel (1903:148–51). The symbol *ṃ* stands for the Kannada *sonne,* pronounced (in this position) as /m/ in modern Kannada.

4. From Ramaswami Aiyar (1936). The author's phonetic symbols are altered to agree with the transcription used above for Kannada.

5. The complicated history of Tulu initial /t c s d j/ is dealt with by Ramaswami Aiyar (1932b). However, he does not clearly distinguish the various Tulu dialects represented in his material. Thus, the stem meaning 'to be entangled' is given as *cikk-, tikk-, śikk-,* and *sikk-,* only the first being distinguished as 'rare sub-dialectal.'

6. Information on the history of **ṟ̤,* and on its modern pronunciation, is given in Krishnamurti (1958b).

2

Sociolinguistic Variation and Language Change

WITH
A. K. RAMANUJAN

1. Introduction

It seems probable that no language is as monolithic as our descriptive grammars sometimes suggest; wherever sufficient data are available, we find diversity within languages on all levels—phonological, grammatical, and lexical. Such diversity can be studied along three synchronic dimensions—geographical, social, and stylistic. The geographical dimension is, of course, the main one which has occupied the attention of dialectologists and which has been presented in dialect atlases. Other types of variation within languages, however, have received less attention. What is here termed the social dimension of linguistic variation is correlated with the socially established identity of the speaker and/or the person addressed or mentioned. Examples are the special linguistic forms used in Nootka to speak to or about children, fat people, dwarfs, hunchbacks, etc. (Sapir 1915); cases of separate men's and women's speech, as in Koasati (Haas 1944); and the cases, familiar from our own society, where speech differences are correlated with the speaker's social status. The term 'sociolinguistic variation' may be applied to cases such as these, and in addition to those where linguistic variation is correlated not with the identity of persons, but with other factors in the social context. These are the factors we have called stylistic. Linguistic styles determined by such factors range from the special war-path speech of the Chiricahua Apache (Opler and Hoijer 1940) to the written styles appropriate to particular literary contexts in societies like our own. Included here also are differences between formal and informal styles of speaking. Although these occur, perhaps, in most languages of the world, some speech communities such as those of Arabic and Modern Greek show such a marked difference between formal and informal style as to produce a kind of bidialectism which Ferguson (1959) has named DIGLOSSIA.

The study of all these varieties of sociolinguistic variation has proved especially fruitful in the South Asian area (India, Pakistan, Ceylon), and a volume recently published (Ferguson and Gumperz 1960) has dealt with several aspects of the subject. On the one hand, clear-cut social dialects are found to be associated with the caste system of Hindu society, and these 'caste dialects' constitute one important field for investigation. On the other hand, many Indian languages have formal and informal styles which are differentiated to the point of diglossia. However, since most published works on South Asian languages concentrate on high-caste dialects or formal style, adequate data on differences of caste dialect and on diglossia, as well as on relationships between the two phenomena, are still lacking.

In the Dravidian languages of South India, we find sociolinguistic factors organized into at least two contrasting patterns. In Tamil and Kanarese (and probably also in Telugu and Malayalam), there are classic cases of diglossia. The formal or literary style is used by educated persons in writing and in public address; it varies only slightly with the social class or place of origin of the person using it. Contrasting with this is an informal or colloquial style, showing much greater internal diversity. Differences correlated with the regional and caste background come to the fore in this informal style, although the speech of the educated may be somewhat more uniform than that of the uneducated. An entirely different pattern is found in the Tulu speech community, occupying a small area on the western coast of South India, and probably also in the area of the Kodagu or Coorg language, farther inland. Here we find Hindu societies comparable to those in the rest of South India, but lacking a tradition of written literature in the native tongue. The social functions which are elsewhere served by a formal style of the local languages are here served by the formal variety of Kanarese. Tulu is, to be sure, sometimes written in Kanarese script for informal purposes, but the language is not the customary medium either for education or for a literary tradition. Dialect divisions corresponding to regional differences and caste differences do occur in Tulu, however, just as in the informal styles of Kanarese or Tamil.

The question then arises: What processes have operated to bring about the differences that exist between modern caste dialects? If forms of the present-day dialects are compared with earlier forms of Dravidian speech, it is apparent that some modern forms represent retentions of earlier ones, while others represent innovations. It has been claimed that linguistic innovation in general comes from the lower social levels; thus a recent paper speaks of 'la langue populaire, riche en innovations, qui a pour elle le grand nombre, et la langue des classes aisées, qui est plus conservatrice' (Schogt 1961:91). On the other hand, it has also been argued that phonetic change, and perhaps linguistic change in general, are initiated by the upper social strata, in order to 'maintain a prestige-marking difference' from the lower strata (Joos 1952:229). The lower class is said to narrow the gap again by imitation, forcing the upper class to innovate still more. Thus language change is viewed as a 'protracted pursuit of an elite by an envious mass, and consequent "flight" of the elite' (Fischer 1958:52). The information available on Indian caste dialects can be used to test such views. An investigation of material from Kanarese, and to a lesser extent from Tulu (Bright 1960a, 1960b) reached the following conclusions: (1) It is inadequate to operate simply in terms of 'change'; changes must be classified as phonological, grammatical, or lexical, and as involving loan materials or native materials. (2) In a comparison of a Brahmin dialect of Kanarese with a middle-caste Non-Brahmin dialect (the abbreviations B and NB will be used hereafter), the B dialect showed innovation on the more conscious levels of phonological and lexical borrowing and of semantic change, while the NB dialect showed changes on the less conscious levels of native phonology and morphology. (3) However, in similar study of Tulu, B and NB dialects showed phonological change in similar degrees; the data then at hand were insufficient for the study of other types of change in Tulu.

In an effort to account for the difference between the Kanarese case and the Tulu case, it was hypothesized that it might be due to the existence of a separate formal style in Kanarese, especially as actualized in the written language. That is, the greater literacy of Kanarese Brahmins was seen as a force counteracting tendencies to change in their dialect—the 'frozen' phonology and grammar of the literary language serving to retard the unconscious processes of change to which speech is normally subject. Tulu Brahmin speech, on the other hand, having no written Tulu tradition to affect it, has been subject to changes of the same type that have operated in the NB dialects of Tulu. In more general terms, it is suggested that literacy, wherever it is present in human societies, acts as a brake on processes of linguistic change. This suggestion has recently been supported by a study of Latin legal terminology over a 2000-year period. This study finds an unusually high retention rate in legal vocabulary, and concludes that 'since these materials have been selected within an area where total literacy is a primary and integral necessity in the communicative process, it seems reasonable to conclude that it is to be reckoned with in language change through time and may be expected to retard the rate of vocabulary change' (Zengel 1962:138–39).

It is clear that further study of South Asian caste dialects is desirable in order to establish more clearly the role of literacy in linguistic change. To this end, we have now examined data on caste dialects of Tamil, a language with an exceptionally long literary tradition; at the same time, an expanded body of Tulu data has been taken into consideration. The following sections present our findings on these two language communities.

2. Tamil

The majority of publications on Tamil deal exclusively with the formal style of the language, as manifested in the writing system. Colloquial Tamil, in its various geographical and social dialects, has received attention in publications of Vinson (1895), Matthews (1942), and Jothimutthu (1956); but these works suffer from lack of organization, and they fail to give clear geographical and social identifications of their data. More systematic discussions have been presented by Bloch (1910), Shanmugam Pillai (1960), Zvelebil (1959, 1960a, 1961), and the present authors (1962). The work done to date, however, has barely scratched the surface of the subject, and generalizations about Tamil dialectology are still risky.

With these qualifications in mind, we have nevertheless attempted to find general features distinguishing B from NB dialects of Tamil, and to ascertain which social group plays the innovating role in each case. B data have been obtained from Ayyangar and Ayyar informants, NB data have been obtained from members of Vellala, Nadar, Chettiar, and Christian communities. The historical perspective is provided by considering the Literary Tamil form (which is usually, though not always, historically prior to the colloquial form), the cognates in other Dravidian languages (by reference to Burrow and Emeneau 1961), and the forms which loanwords have in their source languages. The comparisons made are divided into those involving (1) vocabulary, (2) phonology, and (3) morphology; syntactic comparisons are yet to be carried out.*

2.1. Caste differences in Ta. vocabulary may be classified into two types. In the first type, one caste has a loanword and the other has a native word, e.g. B *jalõ* 'water' (Skt. *jala-*), *tīrtõ* 'drinking water' (Skt. *tīrtha-*), *taṇṇi* 'water not for drinking' (native), as against NB *taṇṇi* 'water in general'. In most of the cases noted, it is B which has innovated by introducing the loanword; a contrary case occurs, however, in B *āmbaḍeyā* 'husband', NB *puruṣẽ* (Skt. *puruṣa-*). In a second type of vocabulary, both castes have native terms, e.g. B *tūngu,* NB *orangu* 'sleep'. The B form also has the meaning 'hang' (intransitive), which is apparently the original sense; cf. the corresponding transitive *tūkku* 'lift', and Ka. *tūgu* 'weigh'. The NB form reflects LTa. *uraṅku* and other Dravidian forms meaning 'sleep'. Here B has innovated through semantic shift where NB has not; our sample contains no cases of the opposite possibility. There are, however, cases where the two dialects differ without evidence that one has innovated more than the other, e.g. B *alambu,* NB *kaluvu* 'wash', both apparently descended without change of meaning from PDr. stems.

*Abbreviations used below are Ta. for Tamil, LTa. for Literary Tamil, Ka. for Kanarese, PDr. for Proto-Dravidian, and Skt. for Sanskrit.

2.2. Phonological comparisons of B and NB again may be classified into two types. The first type is that of loanwords, in which B frequently preserves non-native phonology, while NB assimilates them to the native pattern, e.g. B *svāmi,* NB *sāmi, cāmi* (Skt. *svāmin-*). At the same time, B is prone to hypercorrections in loanwords, such as *jīni* 'sugar' (NB *cīni,* from Hindi *cīni*), and *krāfu* 'haircut' (NB *krāppu,* from English 'crop'), where the foreign sounds /j/ and /f/ are erroneously introduced. The second type of phonological comparison involves native words, where the differences found between caste dialects are most clearly typified by the cases where B has /r̤/ while NB has /r̤/ inconsistently varying with /y/ (in northern areas) or /ḷ/ (in southern areas); e.g. B *vār̤epppar̤ō̃* 'banana' as against NB forms like *vār̤eppaḷō̃, vāḷeppar̤ō̃,* and *vāḷeppaḷō̃.* The overall picture thus shows B as innovator in the introduction of foreign phonemes, sometimes in etymologically unpredictable places. NB, on the other hand, innovates in native material, although the result (at least for educated speakers) is often free variation between older and newer forms, rather than complete replacement of the older.

2.3. Morphological differences between B and NB mostly involve varying shapes of morphemes, not all of which can be explained by the regular phonemic correspondences. An example is B *-du,* NB *-ccu* 'it' (subject of verb), as in B *vandudu,* NB *vanduccu* 'it came' (LTa. *vantatu*). In this case it appears that the NB form represents an analogic extension of the ending found in both B and NB *pōccu* 'it went', *āccu* 'it became' (LTa. *pōyiṟṟu, āyiṟṟu*). In this, as in other examples, NB plays the innovating role. In some other examples, to be sure, B and NB seem to have innovated equally, but in different directions, as when the present tense marker (LTa. *-kiṟ*) becomes *-h* in some NB dialects, but *-r* in B; e.g. B *paṇrā̃,* NB *paṇṇuhā̃* 'he does' (LTa. *paṇṇukiṟāṉ*). But no clear case has been noted in which B has innovated while NB remains conservative.

2.4. The examination of Tamil materials which has been carried out so far shows a situation similar to that previously noted for Kanarese. Neither dialect has a monopoly of innovations in any part of the structure, and yet tendencies are discernible: on the part of B, toward greater use of foreign vocabulary, foreign phonology, and semantic shifts; on the part of NB, toward shifts in native phonology and in morphology.

3. Tulu

Published data on Tulu are found in Brigel (1872), Ramaswami Aiyar (1932a, 1932b, 1936), and Krishnamurti (1958b). These sources do not, unfortunately, distinguish regional dialects, so that there is difficulty in separating regional variations from social variations. This problem has been solved in part by checking with three Tulu speakers.

3.1. The comparisons between B and NB dialects of Tulu can be classified as were those of Tamil. Thus we have: (1) vocabulary differences involving loanwords, such as B *puruṣe* 'husband' (Skt. *puruṣa-*), NB *kaṇḍane* (cognate with Ta. *kaṇṭaṉ*, Ka. *gaṇḍa*); (2) vocabulary differences involving native words, such as B *jōvu, jēvu* 'girl', NB *poṇṇu*. The B form means 'child' in some NB dialects, and can be compared with Parji *cēpal*, Ollari *sēpal* 'boy'; the NB form is cognate with Ta. *peṇ* 'woman, girl'. A semantic shift is evident in the B usage. In both these types of correspondence only the B dialect is found to innovate, either by loans from Sanskrit, Hindi, or Kannada, or by semantic shifts of native terms.

3.2. Phonological correspondences are also of two types. (1) Some cases involve loan phonology, as when B aspirated stop corresponds to NB unaspirated stop. Some of these cases are loans from Indo-Aryan, e.g. B *gandha*, NB *ganda* 'fragrance' (Skt. *gandha-*). In other cases, however, B forms with aspiration may be traced to PDr., which had no distinctive aspiration: e.g. B *chaḷi*, NB *caḷi* 'cold' (cf. Ta. *caḷi*). The B aspiration in such cases presumably originates as a hypercorrect pronunciation. (2) Other cases involve native phonology, such as B /s/, NB /t/ from PDr. **c*, as in B *sikk-*, NB *tikk-* 'be obtained' (cf. Ta. *cikku*). The B form may be regarded as the more conservative, especially since PDr. **c* probably included sibilant allophones (as in many modern Ta. dialects). Five other sound correspondences have been noted in which NB shows greater innovation. But we also have a smaller number of cases where the opposite is true, such as the correspondence of B /ē/ to NB /yā/ where PDr. appears to have had **yā*, as in B *ēnɯ*, NB *yānɯ* 'I' (cf. Ta. *yāṇ*). It thus appears that both B and NB have innovated in phonology, with the NB dialect showing the greater number of innovations. The B dialect, however, shows one special kind of innovation, the introduction of the foreign element of aspiration.

3.3. Morphological correspondences between B and NB Tulu are more difficult to deal with historically, since we have no writing system to reflect older forms, and no full reconstruction of PDr. morphology has yet been made. Certain correspondences do yield to investigation, however, such as the one between B *-no,* NB *-da,* Genitive suffix with 'rational' nouns; thus we find B *āṇɯ-no,* NB *āṇɯ-da* 'of the boy' (cf. Ta. *āḷ-iṉ,* with cognate stem). With 'irrational' nouns Tulu has B *-nte,* Nb *-da;* apparently NB has generalized the dental suffix so as to apply to all types of noun. On the other hand, we find a corresondence between B *-i,* NB *-a,* Present Participle marker, as in B *barpi,* NB *barpa* 'coming'; the NB form agrees with other Dravidian languages, as in Ta. *varu-kiṉṟ-a,* Ka. *bar-uv-a* 'coming'.

3.4. In the morphological comparisons, as in the phonological ones, both B and NB are found to innovate. In summary, the Tulu evidence shows the Brahmins as chief innovators in the more conscious varieties of change—semantic shift, lexical borrowing, and phonological borrowing. In the less conscious processes of phonological and morphological change involving native materials, both B and NB dialects innovate.

4. Conclusion

We feel that the evidence so far examined supports the hypothesis that upper and lower class dialects innovate independently of one another, and in two ways, here labelled conscious and unconscious. Of these types of change, the more conscious variety is regularly the mark of the upper class dialect. The less conscious changes apparently may affect both upper and lower dialects, as seen in the Tulu case; but in Kanarese and Tamil, where there is widespread literacy among Brahmins, the formal written style seems to have retarded the less conscious processes of innovation. A study of the Kodagu language, which like Tulu lacks a literary tradition, would be extremely valuable for the further testing of this hypothesis.

The importance of sociolinguistic factors in language history has recently been pointed up by Hoenigswald (1960:55) and by Schogt (1961). We feel that further investigation of social dialects in the South Asian context can contribute much to understanding the mechanisms of linguistic change.

3

Dravidian Metaphony

1. Introduction

The development of South Dravidian phonology has shown, through its entire recorded and reconstructable history, extensive vocalic assimilation of the type which is known as metaphony, umlaut, or vowel mutation.[1] Specifically, the vowels of radical (word-initial) open syllables have become lower when the following syllable contains the low vowel *a*. The points to be made in this paper are four. (1) This process is reflected in all modern South Dravidian languages, though it is obscured in the literary dialects of Tamil and Malayalam by a change of an opposite, dissimilatory type. (2) The process, which in its earliest form affected only high short vowels, has spread in some languages to affect other vowels, including long ones. (3) This enlarged scope of the process has in some cases produced new phonemic distributions and expanded phonemic inventories. (4) The process has parallels in non-Dravidian languages of South Asia, raising the possibility that a linguistic area or Sprachbund, made up of languages displaying metaphony, may be recognized in the Indian subcontinent.

2. Metaphony of *I* and *U*

The earlier history of this type of assimilation, as traced by Krishnamurti[2] has involved the following steps.

2.1. PDR TO PSDR.[3] Proto-Dravidian had short and long vowels of qualities **i *e *a *o *u* in radical syllables. As Proto-South-Dravidian split off, short **i* and **u,* in the environment before single consonant plus **a,* changed to **e* and **o* respectively, merging with original **e* and **o* of Proto-Dravidian, and neutralizing the contrast of high vs. mid vowels in the stated environment. Examples are PDr. **iṭ-* > PSDr. **eṭ-aṟu* 'stumble' (cf. PSDr. **iṭ-i* 'hit against'), PDr. **pur-* > PSDr. **por-ay* 'layer'. The date of this change is unknown, but must have considerably preceded the period of the early Tamil literature, which dates from around the 3rd century BC.

2.2. PSDR TO THE MODERN LITERARY LANGUAGES. As Proto-South-Dravidian broke up into Telugu, Kannada, and Tamil (with Malayalam as a later offshoot from Tamil), **e* and **o* were maintained in the first two languages. But in Literary Tamil and Malayalam, these vowels, in the environment before *C*a,* changed to *i* and *u* respectively. The neutralization of high vs. mid short vowels in this environment still obtained, then, after the change. Thus PSDr. **eṭ-aṟu* 'stumble', became LTa. *iṭ-aṟu* (cf. OKa. *eḍ-aṟu*), PSDr. **por-ay* 'layer' became LTa. *pur-ai* (cf. OKa. *por-e*). However, as Krishnamurti notes (465), there are a number of unexpected survivals of **e* and **o* in Old Tamil literature, and these probably derive from Old Tamil dialects where the dissimilatory shift did not occur. Thus Tolkāppiyam, the early Tamil grammar, has *peṭ-ai* 'hen' (and so does modern Tamil), instead of expected **piṭ-ai.*[4]

2.3. A SPECIAL DEVELOPMENT IN KANNADA. In Kanarese, by the 8th century AD, radical short *e* and *o,* in the environment before single consonant plus high vowel *i* or *u,* were raised to *i* and *u* respectively (cf. Sreekantaiya 1939). Thus PDr. **eli* 'rat' > Ka. *ili* (cf. Ta. *eli,* Te. *eluka*), PDr. **poṭi* 'powder' > Ka. *puḍi* (cf. Ta. *poṭi,* Te. *poḍi*). However, this assimilation—in the opposite direction from that described in §2.1—seems not to have occurred in all dialects, since many doublets are found like **ed-ir* 'opposite' > OKa. *id-ir, ed-ir* (Gai 1946; cf. modern Ka. *eduru;* cf. Ta. *et-ir,* Te. *ed-uru*).

2.4. MID VOWELS IN TAMIL. As Krishnamurti notes (468), present-day colloquial Tamil and Malayalam frequently show mid vowels *e* and *o* before C*a,* like Kannada or Telugu, but unlike Literary Tamil and Malayalam. We may explain this by assuming that the same metaphonic change that occurred in Proto-Dravidian times has repeated itself—and under exactly the same environmental conditions—or, more reasonably, we may assume that these mid vowels have been preserved ever since the Proto-South-Dravidian period in some spoken varieties of Tamil. The evidence for various Tamil dialects is as follows.

2.4.1. **e* > *e*. The presence of *e,* representing PSDr. **e* before **a,* is attested for all reported dialects of colloquial Tamil.[5] Typical examples of literary-colloquial differences are LTa. *kiṟ̈avi* 'old woman', CTa. *keḷavi;* LTa. *vilai* 'price', CTa. *vele;* LTa. *vicam* 'poison', CTa. *vešõ* (< Skt. *viṣa-*); LTa. *civappu* 'red', CTa. *šehappu.*[6] In some localities, *e* is especially common before LTa. *ṟ* and *r;* typical cases are LTa. *tiṟakka* 'to open', CTa. *terakka;* LTa. *piṟanta* 'being born', CTa. *peranda.*[7] Counter-examples, where a following double consonant preserves PDr. **i,* are LTa. *miṉṉal* 'lightning', CTa. *minnal;* LTa. *pittaḷai* 'brass', CTa. *pittaḷe.* It appears, however, that all reported dialects have some forms in which, even in the expected position, **e* does not occur. Some of these cases may result from informants' efforts to bring their speech closer to the literary standard—the effect which Friedrich (1961:165) has aptly called 'orthographic dazzle'. Frequently, however, I have definitely confirmed the existence of such forms in the colloquial usage of informants. These cases presumably reflect long-established mixture of regional or social dialects; examples (from a Madras Brahmin speaker) are *višayõ* 'subject' (LTa. *vicayam* < Skt. *viṣaya-*), *sila* 'a few' (LTa. *cila*). All colloquial dialects apparently retain PDr. **i* in forms like *ivẽ* 'this man', *ivã* 'this woman', *ivar* 'this person (polite)', *ivango* 'these people' (LTa. *ivaṉ, ivaḷ, ivar, ivarkaḷ*); the expected change would produce forms homonymous with *evẽ* 'which man?' (LTa. *evaṉ*), etc.[8]

2.4.2. **o > o*. The preservation of PSDr. **o* is similarly attested in all the dialects examined. Typical literary-colloquial comparisons are LTa. *uṭaṉē* 'immediately', CTa. *oḍane;* LTa. *kuṟantai* 'child', CTa. *koḷande;* LTa. *kulai* 'killing', CTa. *kole;* LTa. *uṉakku* 'to you', CTa. *onakku.*[9] Even in the Ceylonese data, where *o* is least reported, we find *onakku* 'to you' and *tovakkam* 'start' (LTa. *tuvakkam;* see Zvelebil 1963c, M. Kanapathi Pillai 1955).

2.5. Irregular cases. It should be noted that the data contain scattered cases of colloquial Tamil *e* and *o* where the usual environmental conditions are not met, and where historical **i* and **u* are expected. Examples are Erode *veṭṭu* 'having left it' (LTa. *viṭṭu*), Tuticorin *nennu* 'having stood' (LTa. *niṉṟu*), Erode *soṭṭu* 'having burned' (LTa. *cuṭṭu;* Zvelebil 1963c), and Jaffna *pottaham* 'book' (LTa. *pustakam;* K. Kanapathi Pillai 1958). Such cases are too scant to permit any explanatory generalizations at this time.[10]

2.6. Malayalam. The preservation of PSDr. **e* and **o* in colloquial Malayalam, contrasting with literary *i* and *u* before *Ca,* is attested by Ramaswami Aiyar (1927), who gives the following examples: lit. *vila* 'price', clq. *vela;* lit. *iṭam* 'place', clq. *eṭam;* lit. *piraḷuka* 'to be smeared', clq. *peraḷuka;* lit. *vitakkyuka* 'to sow', clq. *vetakkyuka;* lit. *uṟakkyuka* 'to be stranded', clq. *oṟakkyuka;* lit. *uṭayuka* 'to break', clq. *oṭayuka.*

2.7. Kota. Among the nonliterary languages of South India, Kota agrees with Kanarese and Telugu in retaining PSDr. **e* and **o* before **Ca,* although the conditioning **a* is usually lost in Kota.[11] Examples are as follows:[12] Ta. *niḻal* 'shade', Ko. *nerl,* Ka. *neḻal* (3046); Ta. *piṟa* 'be born', Ko. *perv-,* Ka. *peṟe* (3622); Ta. *urai* 'be ground', Ko. *orv-,* Ka. *ore* (572); Ta. *uṭai* 'break', Ko. *oṛv-,* Ka. *oḍe* (799).

2.8. TODA. The extremely complex developments of Toda vowels have been discussed by Emeneau (1963:26–36). Most of the rules which can be stated are subject to the listing of numerous exceptions; however, some general tendencies can be noted. Toda usually agrees with Kanarese, Telugu, and Kota in retaining the qualities of PSDr. **e* before *C*a;* though Toda, like Kota, normally loses the conditioning vowel **a*. In 34 cases of PSDr. **e*C*a* which were examined, 27 showed Toda *e,* as in the following examples: Ta. *niṟai* 'become full', To. *neṟ-*, Ka. *nere* (3049); Ta. *iṟai* 'scatter', To. *eṟ-,* Ka. *eṟe* (735). However, among 22 cases of PSDr. **o*C*a,* ten showed Toda *wa,* as in the following examples: Ta. *urai* 'be ground', To. *warf-*, Ka. *ore* (572); Ta. *cura* 'flow', Ko. *corv-*, To. *twar-* (2353). The exceptions to the general rule involve five cases of Toda *wï* and scattered instances of *o, ï, u,* and *ü*. Perhaps the most we can say of these data is that Toda tends to an open rather than a close vowel in its reflexes of PSDr. **o* before *C*a*.

2.9. KODAGU. The development of vowels in Kodagu (Coorg) has also been described by Emeneau (1963:36–40). This language agrees with Kota and Kanarese in preserving PSDr. **e* and **o* before *C*a*. Examples: Ta. *iraṇṭu* 'two', Ka. *eraḍu,* Kod. *-eraṇḍï* (401); Ta. *ciṟai* 'to restrain; a tank', Ka. *kere,* Kod. *kere* (1648); Ta. *putai* 'be buried', Ka. *pode,* Kod. *poda-* (3686); Ta. *kuẓal* 'tube', Ka. *koẓal,* Kod. *koḷa* (1511). It should be noted, however, that PSDr. **e* becomes Kodagu *ë* before retroflexes, as in Ta. *iṭai* 'left (hand)', Ka. *eḍa,* Kod. *ëḍate* (381). When **e* in this position is also preceded by a labial, it changes further to Kod. *o,* as in Ta. *viḷakku* 'lamp', Ka. *beḷaku,* Kod. *boḷakï* (4524).

2.10. TULU. The data available for Tulu, as was pointed out by Ramaswami Aiyar (1936:432–33), show both *i* and *e* where PSDr. **e* precedes *C*a,* and both *u* and *o* for PSDr. **o*. The dictionary of Männer (1886) gives some forms with high vowels, e.g., *simè* 'eyelash' (cf. Ta. *imai*) and *pudelï* 'bush' (Ta. *putal*); and some forms only with low vowels, e.g., *eḷe* 'young' (Ta. *iḷai*) and *posa* 'new' (Ta. *putu*). It also lists many doublets such as *kirè* ~ *kerè* 'tank' (Ta. *ciṟai*) and *munè* ~ *monè* 'point' (Ta. *muṉai*).

In attempting to understand the development of these vowels in Tulu, it is necessary first of all to realize that the language has borrowed heavily from Kanarese; thus many occurrences of *e* and *o* are suspect of being Kanarese loans. This is the case in several of the examples cited above: we have Ka. *eḷe* 'young', Tu. *eḷe*; Ka. *kere* 'tank', Tu. *kerè*; Ka. *mone* 'point', Tu. *monè*. There are other cases, however, where Tu. and Ka. forms are different enough that we can reject the possibility of borrowing: Ka. *ime* 'eyelash', Tu. *simè*; Ka. *podar* 'bush', Tu. *pudelï*. It is from words of this type that we may hope to establish the regular development of the Tulu vowels.

But even after possible Kanarese loans are eliminated from consideration, Männer's data still show both high and mid vowels, as in *buḷe-* ~ *boḷe-* 'ripen' (Ta. *viḷai,* Ka. *beḷe;* Tulu here shows rounding after the initial labial). Presumably such doublets reflect dialect differences, but these are not explained by Männer. My own data from Tulu informants suggest that it is a difference in social dialect which is involved, and specifically that the forms with mid vowels are characteristic of the Brahmin dialects, while the forms with high vowels are characteristic of non-Brahmin speech.[13] Examples are Br. *kelanji* 'a fly', NBr. *kilenji;* Br. *oḷeyi* 'inside', NBr. *ulayi;* Br. *boḷe-* 'ripen', NBr. *bule-*. But there are also cases where both Brahmin and non-Brahmin dialects have a high vowel, as in *irè* 'leaf' (Ta. *ilai,* Ka. *ele*), and fresh field work will be necessary before the developments are clarified.

3. Metaphony of Nonhigh Vowels

Some South Dravidian dialects show a slightly different type of metaphony, namely the lowering of MID vowels when a nonhigh vowel occurs in the following syllable (even when more than one consonant intervenes). In this process, instances of *e* display the quality [ɛ] or [æ], and instances of *o* have the quality [ɔ]. In many cases, this development has not yet produced any phonemic contrasts; in other cases, full-fledged phonemic split has taken place.

3.1. TAMIL. There are reports of metaphony affecting both short and long mid vowels in some dialects of Tamil, but mainly on the allophonic level, as follows.

3.11. The development of a metaphonic distinction between short [e] and [ɛ] is only weakly attested. Zvelebil notes that colloquial Tamil *e* (as well as long *ē*) has allophones of quality [ɛ] and [e], the latter occurring 'most probably when followed by *i* and *i:* in the next syllable' (1963b:227). His example is [teriya:ðï] 'is not known', but he also writes [čɛḍi] 'a plant'. My own impression is that for most speakers *e* has a phonetic norm [ɛ], but with some free variation toward [e] when a high vowel occurs in the following syllable.[14]

3.12. Metaphony operates in several dialects to differentiate long [e·] from [ɛ·] or [æ·]. My clearest examples are from a Vellore dialect which systematically has [e·] when a high vowel follows, [ɛ·] elsewhere; e.g. *v*[e·]*ṇū* 'is wanted' vs. *v*[ɛ·]*ṇā* 'is not wanted', *k*[e·]*ṭṭu* 'having asked' vs. *k*[ɛ·]*ṭṭē* 'I asked', *v*[e·]*ṣṭi* 'a garment' vs. *v*[ɛ·]*le* 'work'. In the speech of my colleague A. K. Ramanujan, representing Madras Brahmin usage, [æ·] occurs in such cases only if *v* precedes, but a few contrasts with [e·] have arisen because of vowel change in the following syllables; e.g. *vēkamāy* > *v*[æ·]*hamā* 'quickly' vs. *vēkukiṟatu* > *v*[e·]*haradu* 'it's cooking'.[15] The dialect data collected by Zvelebil give the form *v*[æ·]*le* 'work' from Madurai, but no information on possible contrasts (1959:290). Finally, we may note that [æ·] seems to have changed further to [a·] in some cases, since Zvelebil reports *vēṇṭām* > *vāṇä* 'isn't wanted' from Madras. (1959:587).

3.13. A metaphonic relation between short [o] and [ɔ] is noted by Zvelebil (1963b:228), and has been observed in my Vellore data mentioned above, but with no evidence of any developing contrast. The data show [o] when high vowels follow, as in *k*[o]*ṟ̈i* 'creeper', *m*[o]*ggu* 'bud', and [ɔ] elsewhere, as in *k*[ɔ]*ḍe* 'umbrella', *m*[ɔ]*ḷḷo* 'slowly'.

3.14. A phonetic distinction between long [o·] and [ɔ·] is not mentioned by Zvelebil, but is plainly observable in the Vellore dialect already referred to. Before high vowels, [o·] occurs, as in *p*[o·]*hū* 'it will go', *k*[o·]*vil* 'temple'; before other vowels, [ɔ·] occurs, as in *p*[ɔ·]*rā* 'he goes', *k*[ɔ·]*ṇal* 'crooked'. There is no evidence of contrast, and the phenomenon has not been reported so far from other Tamil dialects.

3.2. TODA. In Toda **ō* (but not **ē*) shows effects of **a* in the next syllable. As stated by Emeneau (1963:28), 'Otherwise than after *p-*, **ō* > *wa·* when the next syllable (the last in the word) has **-ay;* otherwise, **ō* > *wï·*.' An example is Ta. *kōṭai* 'west wind, summer', To. *kwa·ṛ* 'monsoon, year'.

3.3. KANARESE. The modern colloquial language displays, in some of its dialects, metaphony not only of mid /e ē o ō/, but also of the near-mid [ə] allophone of /a̱/. In some areas, nothing more than allophonic distinctions result; in others, five new vowel phonemes develop, three short and two long.

3.31. In the Bangalore Brahmin dialect which was the basis for my monograph on Kanarese (Bright 1958a), some speakers have two allophones for /a/ in initial syllables: [ə] when the following syllable contains a high vowel, and [ʌ] elsewhere, as in *t*[ə]*ndu* 'having brought' vs. *t*[ʌ]*nde* 'father'. However, as Sreekantaiya has pointed out (1940), there are closely related dialects in which the closed [ə] has been analogically generalized, so that alongside of *t*[ə]*ndu* 'having brought' there is also *t*[ə]*nde* 'I brought', contrasting with *t*[ʌ]*nde* 'father'.

3.32. The influence of metaphony has gone much farther, however, in the Dharwar dialect of Kanarese as reported by Hiremath (1961:1–10). The processes which have operated there may be reconstructed as follows. At one time, the vowels /e ē a o ō/ had the closed allophones [e e· ə o o·] when a following syllable contained a high vowel, and open allophones [æ æ· ʌ ɔ ɔ·] when the following syllable contained a nonhigh vowel. Subsequently, however, this dialect changed nonhigh /e/ to high /i/ in final position. As a result, the allophonic differences between closed and open vowels acquired phonemic status. The development is shown in Table 3.1.[16]

3.33. A different type of vocalic assimilation, found in medieval and modern Kanarese, involves medial vowels: *i* > *u* before *u,* and *u* > *i* before *e*. Examples are *usiru* 'breathe' > *usuru, tiḷipu* 'make known' > *tiḷupu* (cf. *tiḷi* 'be known'), *aḍuge* 'cooking' < *aḍige* (Sreekantaiya 1939:771). We have here, then, assimilation involving fronting rather than height, going beyond the definition of metaphony presented above.

TABLE 3.1

Literary Kanarese		*Earlier Dharwar Kanarese*	*Present Dharwar Kanarese*
keḍu	'spoil'	*[keḍu]	*keḍu*
mere	'appear'	*[mære]	*mæri*
pēṭi	'harmonium'	*[pe·ṭi]	*pēṭi*
pēṭe	'market'	*[pæ·ṭe]	*pǣṭi*
kari	'fry'	*[kəri]	*kəri*
kare	'call'	*[kʌri]	*kari*
koḍu	'give'	*[koḍu]	*koḍu*
kore	'cut'	*[kɔre]	*kɔri*
kōṭi	'crore'	*[ko·ṭi]	*kōṭi*
kōṭe	'fort'	*[kɔ·ṭe]	*kɔ̄ṭi*

3.4. TULU. There is no evidence of metaphony affecting mid vowels in the published literature, nor in the speech of several Tulu informants who have been interviewed; although there is a contrast between /e/ and /ɛ/, it occurs only in word-final position. However, one informant, a Brahmin from Mangalore (bilingual in Konkani and Kannada) differentiates long /ē ō/ from /ɛ̄ ɔ̄/ according to the following pattern. The closed vowels occur when a high vowel /i u ï e/ follows, as in *bēri* 'root', *pōpe* 'he's going', and also in some Indo-Aryan loans, e.g. *dēsa* 'country', *kōpa* 'anger'. The open vowels occur when a low vowel /ɛ a/ follows, as in *bɛ̄te* 'different', *pɔ̄pɛ* 'I'm going'; the examples here also include some Indo-Aryan loans, such as *bɛ̄ga* 'fast' (Skt. *vega,* Ka. *bēga*). It is not known how common these distinctions are among Tulu speakers.

4. General Metaphony: Telugu

As has been described in the most detail by Kelley (1959, 1963), all the vowels of colloquial Telugu, both short and long, are found in closed varieties before high vowels and in open varieties before low vowels. The loss of the conditioning vowels through the operation of sandhi rules then creates apparent contrasts between [i] and [ɪ], [i·] and [ɪ·], etc. Some examples: [gu·ḍu] 'nest', plural *[gu·ḍu-lu] > [gu·ḷḷu], but [gʊ·ḍɑ] 'basket', plural *[gʊ·ḍɑ-lu] < [gʊḷḷʊ]; [kəmpu] 'a smell', *[kəmpu-a·] > [kəmpa·] 'is it a smell?', but [kɑmpɑ] 'branch', *[kɑmpɑ-a·] > [kɑmpɑ·] 'is it a branch?'; [go·ru] 'fingernail', plural *[go·ru-lu] > [go·ḷḷu], but [gɔḍɑ] 'wall', plural *[gɔ·ḍa-lu] > [gɔ·ḷḷʊ] 'walls'. Rather than doubling the number of vowel phonemes which we recognize for Telugu, however, it is possible to set up a 'long component' or 'covowel' of lowering; Kelley's symbol is /ˆ/. The minimal pairs given above can then be written as /gu·ḷḷu/ 'nests' vs. /gû·ḷḷu/ 'baskets', /kampa·/ 'is it a smell?' vs. /kâmpa·/ 'is it a branch?', and /go·ḷḷu/ 'fingernails' vs. /gô·ḷḷu/ 'walls'.

In addition, Telugu shows less regular processes of vocalic assimilation in nonradical syllables. Three types may be distinguished.

(1) In Old Telugu (11th–14th centuries), the personal suffixes of verbs show 'vowel harmony', having the vowel *i* when the preceding vowel is *i*, but the vowel *u* otherwise. Examples: *vaṇḍ-e-nu* 'he cooked', *vaṇḍ-eḍi-ni* 'he cooks'; *vaṇḍ-iti-ni* 'I cooked', *vaṇḍu-du-nu* 'I cook'. Modern Telugu has new developments in verb inflection which give no occasion for this type of vowel assimilation to operate (Krishnamurti 1961:189–91, 212–14).

(2) The same kind of assimilation appears in the case suffixes of nouns. In Old Telugu, the dative suffix is *-kin* ~ *-kun*, as in *rāmuni-kin* 'to Rama', *gōḍala-kun* 'to the walls'. The alternation is preserved in modern Telugu *-ki* ~ *-ku*. For the accusative case, Old Telugu *-n* becomes modern *-ni* ~ *-nu*, as in *puli-ni* 'tiger', *biḍḍa-nu* 'child' (Arden 1937:63, 382).

(3) In Old Telugu, stem-medial vowels alternate according to a rule that 'In trisyllabic bases, *u* of the second syllable alternates with *i*, when a front vowel (*i* or *e*) occurs in the following syllable', e.g. *aḍugu-cun* 'asking', *aḍig-i* 'having asked'. In modern Telugu, the scope of the alternation is expanded, so that '*u* of the second syllable of disyllabic and trisyllabic bases of the (C)VCVC(V) type becomes *i* before a front vowel and *a* before *a* in the immediately following syllable', yielding not only *aḍig-i* 'having asked' but also *aḍag-a* 'to ask' (Krishnamurti 1961:204, 225).

It will be seen that these developments involve several processes not general in Dravidian: assimilation of fronting, rather than of height; progressive as well as regressive assimilation; and (especially in the change of *u..a* to *a..a*) complete rather than partial assimilation. The domains of these changes have remained restricted, however; e.g. plural *-lu* remains unassimilated, in forms like *strī-lu* 'women'.

5. Central and Northern Dravidian

No comparative phonology of the Central and Northern Dravidian languages has been worked out, so that it is not yet possible to state the extent of vocalic assimilation in these nonliterary languages. Thus Krishnamurti notes that 'Many divergences from the Proto-Dravidian system appear in these languages even in radical vowels, so that one cannot set up regular phonemic correspondences to explain all the material.' But in some cases, at least, these languages seem to reflect Proto-Dravidian vowel qualities, and are accordingly useful in reconstruction: e.g. LTa. *ira* 'beg', Ka. *ere,* Malto *irgr-* 'borrow' can be reconstructed as PDr. **ir-;* LTa. *tiṟa* 'to open', OKa. *teṟe,* Gondi *tarī-* (with *a* < **e*) can be reconstructed as PDr. **teṯ-* (1958a:462–64).

In Kurukh (Oraon), a Central Dravidian language, there are verb stems which show conditioned alternation between *i* and *e, u* and *o.* In some cases, the alternant with the high vowel is followed by a suffix containing a high vowel, as in *eṛ-nā* 'to call', *iṛ-ī* 'she calls', *iṛ-ū* 'habitually calling'; *bong-nā* 'to run', *bung-dī* 'thou runnest' (Grignard 1924:66–67). Neither full descriptive details nor a historical explanation are available at present.

6. Metaphony in Munda

In an attempt to trace the broader history of Dravidian metaphony, the other major language families of India may be examined. In the Munda languages, vocalic assimilation seems to be of little recent importance, but may be discerned in an earlier historical period. Santali is said to have contrasting /e/ and /ɛ/, /o/ and /ɔ/, and a Proto-Munda vowel system containing **e *ɛ *o *ɔ* is reconstructed by Pinnow (1959), but with the qualification that the functional load of the close-open contrast was low (195). This is explained in terms of an earlier system with only two front vowels **i *ɛ,* and two back vowels **u *ɔ,* whereupon it followed 'dass die alten Kombinationen der Vokale des engen Öffnungsgrades *(i, u)* mit solchen des halboffenen Öffnungsgrades *(ɛ, ɔ)* aneinander angeglichen worden sind' (124). It would appear that vowel assimilation in pre-Proto-Munda operated progressively as well as regressively: not only did the vowel sequence **i..a* become *e..a,* but **a..i* also became *a..e*. This contrasts with the Dravidian situation, where metaphony of non-initial vowels has not been notable.

7. Indo-Aryan

Vowel assimilation cannot be said to be widespread in the Indo-Aryan languages. Their earlier history shows numerous examples of changes between high and mid vowel position, but the conditioning factor is the presence of a following consonant cluster. In such an environment, Skt. long vowels became *ĕ* and *ŏ* in Prakrit, and then tended to merge with short *i* and *u* respectively. The records thus show fluctuation between high and mid vowels before consonant groups. Examples: Skt. *kṣetra* 'land' > Pkt. *chĕtta, chitta;* Skt. *nidrā* 'sleep' > Pkt. *ṇĕddā, ṇiddā;* Skt. *oṣṭha* 'lip' > Pkt. *ŏṭṭha, uṭṭha;* Skt. *kūrpara* 'elbow' > Pkt. *kŏppara, kuppara* (Pischel 1957:77–78, 100–102, 104–5; modern languages show the high vowels in some cases, the mid vowels in others.) It is clear that metaphony is not involved in this development.

Several Indo-Aryan languages have contrasts of [e] with [ɛ] or [æ] and of [o] with [ɔ], but metaphony is not necessarily involved. In some varieties of Hindi, the contrast has arisen through the monophthongization of *ai* and *au* to [æ·] and [ɔ·] respectively. Gujerati has contrasting /e ɛ o ɔ/, but the multiple historical origins of these vowels do not include metaphony (Pandit 1955). Contrastive /e æ o ɔ/ are reported for Maithili, in Bihar; but /æ/ and /ɔ/ arise primarily through contractions (Jha 1958:95–96). And in Bhojpuri, also of Bihar, phonetic [ɛ] and [ɔ] are reported, but they seem to involve neither metaphonic origins nor contrastive status as opposed to [e] and [o] (Tiwari 1960:5–6). Surveying the closest Indo-Aryan neighbors of the Dravidian languages, we find no vocalic assimilation reported for Marathi or Oriya. We do find it, however, in four languages: Konkani, Bengali, Assamese, and Singhalese.

7.1. KONKANI. This language, spoken adjacent to the Dravidian area on the west coast of India, has short and long [e] and [o] when a high vowel follows, but [æ] and [ɔ] elsewhere. Examples are [kǣḷǣ] 'banana' vs. [kẽ·ḷĩ·] 'bananas', [bhæt·a·] 'breaks' vs. [bhe·ti] 'broken condition'; and, for the back vowels, [pɔḷɔ] 'pancake' vs. [po·ḷi] 'sweets', [bhɔḷɔ] 'simple (masc.)' vs. [bho·ḷi] 'simple (fem.)'[17] There is no evidence, however, that any phonemic distinction has arisen. The similarity of Konkani metaphony to that found in Kanarese and Tulu—reinforced by the absence of metaphony in Marathi, the closest Indo-Aryan language—make it seem likely that the process has diffused into Konkani from Dravidian sources.

7.2. BENGALI. Far more than any other Indo-Aryan language, Bengali shows sweeping processes of vocalic assimilation, including metaphony, both in the historical development of the language and in the synchronic morphophonemics. Three types of change may be distinguished, following the presentation of Chatterji:[18]

(1) The vowels *i u e* are lowered one step (to *e o æ* respectively) when followed by a vowel other than *i* or *u*. Examples: √*gil* 'swallow' > *gela* 'swallowed', *gele* 'he swallows', *gelo* 'you swallow', but *gili* 'I swallow', *giluk* 'let him swallow'; √*šun* 'hear' > *šona* 'heard' etc., but *šuni* 'I hear'; √*dekh* 'see' > *dækha* 'seen' etc., but *dekhi* 'I see'.

(2) The vowels *e o æ ɔ* are raised one step (to *i u e o* respectively) when followed by one of the high vowels *i* or *u*. Examples: *deši* 'country-made' > *diši,* √*šo* 'lie down' > *šui* 'I lie down' (but *šoe* 'he lies down'), *æk* 'one' but *ekṭi* 'one little thing', *nɔṭ* 'actor' but *noṭi* 'actress'.

(3) The vowel *a* is raised to *e* or *o* when PRECEDED by *i* or *u* respectively. Examples are *kɔritam* 'I used to do' > *kortem, uṭhan* 'courtyard' > *uṭhon.* (It is not clear from the available descriptions when this process takes priority over the process numbered 1.)

Several aspects of these processes are notable. (a) Bengali assimilation, unlike the most widespread Dravidian variety, operates across consonant clusters. (b) Bengali has much more general tendencies to vocalic assimilation—both progressive and regressive, to both high and nonhigh vowels—than do the Dravidian languages, where regressive assimilation to low vowels is the general rule. (c) Bengali assimilation is still a living process, attested in loanwords from both Persian and English; e.g. Persian *hisāb* 'accounts' > *hišeb;* English *Guernsey* > *gɔnji* > *gonji.*

7.3. ASSAMESE. Like its close relative Bengali, Assamese shows vocalic assimilation, though in a less sweeping way. The historical split of *e* and *o* into open and close varieties depending on the following vowel is attested by such pairs of words as *kola* 'black' (Skt. *kōkila*) vs. *kɔla* 'plantain' (Skt. *kadala*), *moh* 'buffalo' (Skt. *mahiṣa*) vs. *mɔh* 'gnat' ((Skt. *maśaka*) (Chatterji 1926:388). Morphophonemically, the same process is reflected in *bɛṭa* 'son' vs. *beṭi* 'daughter', *jol* 'water' vs. *juliya* 'watery' (Kakati 1941:64–66).

7.4. SINGHALESE. Three main types of vocalic assimilation in the historical development of Singhalese are described by Geiger (1938:18–26).

(1) The term 'umlaut' is applied by Geiger to the fronting of *u o a* to *i e ä* when the next syllable contains a front vowel. This occurs only in 'heavy' syllables, i.e. those which have an original long vowel or a short vowel followed by a consonant cluster. Examples: Skt. *sūci* 'needle' > Si. *hidi,* Skt. *kōṭi* 'point' > Si. *keḷa,* Skt. *mandira* 'house' > Si. *mädiri.*

(2) Geiger applies the term 'vowel-assimilation' to cases where a vowel is completely assimilated to the vowel of the following syllable. This takes place in 'light' syllables, i.e. in those where an original short vowel is followed by a single consonant. Examples: Skt. *pipāsā* 'thirst' > Si. *pavas,* Skt. *maṇi* 'germ' > Si. *miṇi,* Skt. *prabuddha* 'awake' > Si. *pubudu.*

(3) Geiger's term 'vowel-levelling' refers to a change whereby sequences of a low and a nonlow vowel (in either order) undergo mutual assimilation, resulting in a sequence of two identical mid vowels. Examples: Skt. *mahilā* 'woman' > Si. *meheli* 'old woman', Skt. *vihāra* 'temple' > Si. *vehera,* Skt. *prasūna* 'flower' > Si. *poson,* Skt. *śmaśāna* 'grave' > Pkt. *susāna* > Si. *sohon.*

These processes are not prominent in the oldest Singhalese documents; they are assigned to a period between the 5th and 10th centuries AD. (Geiger 1900:34–36). It is clear that the most prominent elements of Singhalese assimilation—assimilation of fronting, and COMPLETE assimilation of height—differentiate it from both the general Dravidian and the Bengali developments.

8. Conclusions

We have found processes of vocalic assimilation operating in an area which includes South Dravidian, Munda, and Indo-Aryan languages, and which extends from Assam to Ceylon; one is tempted to recognize a Sprachbund, a linguistic area of the type defined for South Asia by Emeneau.[19] But there are difficulties. In the first place, the Oriya language is a discontinuity in the supposed linguistic area. Furthermore, at least three types of assimilation have to be distinguished. Most of the Dravidian varieties, from the prehistoric period down to the apparently recent developments in Telugu, have involved partial assimilation to the open quality of a following low vowel. But outside of Dravidian, only Konkani fits this limited pattern. In Munda, the pattern is enlarged by the addition of progressive assimilation; in Bengali and Assamese, it is still further enlarged in that assimilation to high vowels also occurs; and in Singhalese, assimilation of fronting, as well as complete (rather than partial) assimilation, make their appearance. Are all of these phenomena related by diffusion, or are they independent developments?

Perhaps a clue is provided by considerations of chronology. Dravidian metaphony, of the relatively limited type described above, seems to have been a live process from prehistoric times to the present, perhaps uninteruptedly in certain social dialects, breaking out into the literary record in scattered times and places, and being most completely revealed only by recent structural studies of spoken usage. By contrast, Munda vowel assimilation seems to have operated only during a limited period; Bengali assimilation is manifested mostly in the recent history of the language; Singhalese assimilation operated during the medieval period of the language, and then stopped. It is possible to hypothesize that each of the non-Dravidian developments represents a period of influence from the Dravidian pattern, followed by a generalization of the pattern to involve such factors as progressive assimilation, raising, fronting, and complete assimilation. By this hypothesis, a linguistic area would indeed be recognized, including most of the eastern and southern parts of the Indian subcontinent. Support for the hypothesis must come from new linguistic data, as well as from material on the nonlinguistic history of India.

NOTES

1. On the term 'metaphony', cf. Blaylock (1965).

2. Krishnamurti (1958a); cf. also Burrow (1940).

3. Abbreviations used in this paper: PDr. Proto-Dravidian, PSDr. Proto-South-Dravidian, Ta. Tamil, LTa. Literary Tamil, CTa. Colloquial Tamil, Ka. Kannaḍa (Kanarese), LKa. Literary Kannaḍa, OKa. Old Kannaḍa, Tu. Tulu, Te. Telugu, Skt. Sanskrit, Pkt. Prakrit, Si. Singhalese, Br. Brahmin, NBr. Non-Brahmin.

4. Alternation of high and mid vowels in such cases is reported from early inscriptional evidence by K. Kanapathi Pillai (1935). I am indebted to Pillai and to the Librarian of the University of London for making this dissertation available to me on microfilm.

5. Such occurrences of mid vowels are reported as characteristic of Colloquial Tamil in general by several sources: Vinson (1895:121–22), Jothimutthu (1956:216), Sethu Pillai (1938–39), Shanmugam Pillai (1960:32–33). Published sources for specific regional dialects follow: Bloch (1910), for Madras, Chidambaram, Kumbakonam, Chingleput, and Tirumangalam; Zvelebil (1959, 1960a, 1963c), for Madras, Erode, Dindigul, Madurai, Ramnad, Tuticorin, Tinnevelly, and Trincomalaee; Zvelebil (1960b), for Jaffna and Trincomalee; K. Kanapathi Pillai (1958), for Jaffna; and M. Kanapathi Pillai (1955:65–69), for Ceylonese Tamil in general. (I have been provided with a copy of this last work through the kindness of Indreni M. Savundranavagam.) Data have also been gathered from informants for the dialects of Madras, Kumbakonam, Vellore, Tinnevelly, and Jaffna; I am indebted for such material to Mrs. Nesamani Lazarus, to K. V. Ramanathan, Samuel Z. Koil Pillai, and Shridhar Subramanyam, and especially to A. K. Ramanujan of the University of Chicago. Most of the data studied have been from middle-caste speakers; but the preservation of Proto-Dravidian mid vowels is also well attested in data from Brahmin and Untouchable dialects.

6. Literary Tamil forms are given in the usual transliteration; Colloquial Tamil forms are in phonemic notation. The notation used here is intended to reflect an 'overall pattern' of dialectal phonology; it gives full value to the contrasts introduced by loanwords, viz. *k/g/h, c/j/š/s, ṭ/ḍ, t/d,* and *p/b*. (For discussion of the phonemic problem, and a different decision, cf. Fairbanks 1957). The shapes of the colloquial examples are typical of a wide variety of dialects.

7. Zvelebil's data show *e* mainly in the environment of *ṟ* and *r* in the dialects of Erode, Dindigual, Tuticorin, Tinnevelly, and in the Ceylon dialects. My Tinnevelly informant, however, gave many examples like *eḍadu* 'left (hand)', LTa. *iṭatu; sele* 'few', LTa. *cila*. Similarly, the Ceylonese data contain examples like *cehappu* 'red', LTa. *civappu; eḍai* 'weight', LTa. *iṭai* (K. Kanapathi Pillai 1935:221); *eṟavu* 'bereavement', LTa. *iṟavu* (M. Kanapathi Pillai, 1935:65).

8. Data from Nagercoil presented in Subramoniam (1958) include many cases where the dissimilatory *i* appears (as in the verb lists, 81–92), but also several cases of *e*, e.g. *ele* 'leaf' (14), LTa. *ilai; cevatta* 'reddish' (70), LTa. *civatta*.—It should be noted that there are scattered instances of PDr. **e* yielding *o* in the colloquial dialects—usually, but not always, after a labial consonant—and other cases where it has become *a*. Examples are *moḷahu* 'pepper', LTa. *miḷaku; tora* 'to open', LTa. *tiṟa; kaṟame* 'day of the week', LTa. *kiṟamai*.

9. All forms of the second person oblique pronominal stem (LTa. *uṉ*) commonly show *o* in colloquial Tamil, regardless of the environment following; hence we have LTa. *uṉ* 'you (sg.)', CTa. *õ;* LTa. *unkaḷ* 'you (pl.)', CTa. *onga*.

10. Burrow (1940:290) points to several cases where Kanarese and Telugu show unexpected *e* and *o* before a double consonant, e.g. Ka. *moṭṭe* 'egg' (cf. Ta. *muṭṭai*).

11. All Kota data, as collected by Emeneau, are taken from Burrow and Emeneau (1961), hereafter abbreviated *DED*.

12. Sets of cognates are preceded by the number assigned them in the *DED*. The glosses given here are much abbreviated.

13. Differences between Brahmin and Non-Brahmin Tulu are discussed by Ramaswami Aiyar (1932a, 1936). He does not, however, mention the correspondence of high and mid vowels. For my own data on Tulu, I am indebted to Ramakrishna Adiga, Harihar Rao, Shankar Shetty, and Krishna Shetty; my thanks also go to Charles Richards for data collected by him.

14. Quite different processes seem to have produced a contrast between [e] and [ɛ] in a few dialects. In A. K. Ramanujan's speech (Madras Brahmin), there is a possible word-final contrast between LTa. *ai* > [ɛ] and LTa. *ē, ay*

> [e]. A contrast in Ceylon Tamil is also reported by M. Shanmugam Pillai (1962), esp. 96, but its origins are not clear.

15. The phone [æ·], as introduced by English loanwords, has a well-established foothold in most Tamil dialects; pronounciations like *bǣŋku* 'bank' are widespread.

16. Some of Hiremath's data do not show the expected changes, e.g. *koḍi* 'umbrella' (p. 1) as compared with LKa. *koḍe*. This is presumably due to dialect mixture, reflected also in Hiremath's report of free variation in cases like *bēḍa* ~ *bǣḍa* 'hunter' (p. 3), as compared with LKa. *bēḍa*.

17. Katre (1935:14). The data do not make it clear whether vowel length is contrastive.

18. The diachronic details are provided by Chatterji (1926:387–402). A synchronic description is given by Dimock (1957).

19. Emeneau (1956). I am indebted to Emeneau for his helpful comments on an earlier draft of this paper.

4

Language, Social Stratification, and Cognitive Orientation

Sociolinguistics is a thriving infant, but an infant nevertheless.[1] Thus, the literature is still meager in the subfield dealing with the linguistic correlates of social stratification. In 1956 it was noted that of two review articles on social stratification, 'neither lists any study dealing with language as a status-related factor' (Putnam and O'Hern 1956); and the same comment holds for a similar review article published in 1964 (Murphy 1964). In fact, it is only very recently that any combination of sociological and linguistic sophistication has been brought to bear on the subject. Thus, on the level of linguistic structure or *langue,* we still have no thorough phonological, grammatical, and semantic comparison of even a single pair of class dialects; and on the level of linguistic behavior or *parole,* we still have no 'ethnography of speaking' (to use Hymes' term, 1962) for even the simplest kind of community. Lacking such basic bodies of data, discussion in sociolinguistics must often SUGGEST rather than CLAIM.

Among the more interesting suggestions that have been made are those which point to a relationship within social strata between language and cognitive orientation, using this term to cover such matters as world view, value systems, and other matters of psychological outlook. Here we are dealing with what has been called the concept of linguistic relativity, associated with the name of Benjamin Lee Whorf, but in an extended sense. Whorf was concerned with correlations between world view and linguistic structure; but as has been pointed out by Hymes (1966), we may apply Whorf's concepts also to language behavior, i.e. to the different WAYS that language is used in various societies. Furthermore, although Whorf's comparisons involved widely differing linguistic communities, such as that of the Hopi versus 'Standard Average European', we may equally well undertake comparisons between parts of a single community, such as those parts which are characterized by differing linguistic structures and/or differing patterns of linguistic behavior.

The relations between language, social stratification, and cognitive orientation have been studied most deeply in a series of publications by Bernstein. In these papers, a distinction is made between a 'restricted code', speech which uses relatively limited linguistic resources and is consequently predictable to a high degree, as against an 'elaborated code', which allows a larger number of structural options and shows a correspondingly low level of predictability. In terms of social-psychological correlates, the restricted code is 'status oriented': it 'elicits and progressively strengthens a relatively undifferentiated adherence to the normative arrangements of a local structure' and 'promotes the transmission of social rather than individual symbols'.[2] The elaborated code, on the other hand, is 'person rather than status oriented' (Bernstein 1964:63). Bernstein finds that (in the British context of his work) 'a restricted code is available to ALL members of society'; the middle class learns, in addition, an elaborated code, but 'sections of the lower class population' have access ONLY to the restricted code (60). This difference in code use is said both to reflect and to perpetuate the social-psychological differences between the middle class and the working class.

It is clear that the differences between Bernstein's restricted and elaborated codes are matters of language behavior rather than of language structure: both codes draw on the same grammar, but the elaborated code, for instance, uses a higher percentage of subordinate clauses. The question then remains open as to whether the notion of linguistic relativity may apply to differences of linguistic STRUCTURE between class dialects.

Some of our most detailed and useful data on social dialect comes from India; indeed, we may say that much of the current interest in sociolinguistics derives directly from work on Indian languages. Dialect differences specifically correlated with the caste system of India have been reported widely; the general picture is of a dichotomy between Touchable and Untouchable usage in North India, as against a three-way division in South India between Brahmin, Non-Brahmin, and Untouchable dialects.[3] It should be made clear that caste dialects are independent of the dichotomy between formal and informal styles. It may be true that the higher castes have the opportunity to receive an education more often and thereby to become proficient in the formal style. But formal usage is quite a separate system from high-caste informal usage; it is used in a substantially uniform way by all educated people, whatever their caste background may be.

Descriptions of Indian caste dialects, like other sociolinguistic studies, have usually been organized along another dimension, which corresponds to the divisions of language structure recognized by descriptive linguists. The features usually noted under this heading are phonological, grammatical, and lexical. Under the phonological rubric we may be told, for example, that the Brahmin Kanarese initial /h/ corresponds to Non-Brahmin zero in examples like Brahmin *hālu,* Non-Brahmin *ālu* 'milk'. Under grammar it is explained that Brahmin Kanarese has the locative morpheme *-alli* corresponding to Non-Brahmin *-āgi.* Under lexicon such differences as Brahmin *sinima,* Non-Brahmin *bayskōpu* 'movies' are noted (Bright 1960a).

Most published data of this kind refer mainly to differences of phonological shape between semantically equivalent utterances. That is, both Brahmin and Non-Brahmin dialects have morphemes meaning 'milk, locative, movies'; these morphemes have the differing phonemic shapes *hālu* versus *ālu, -alli* versus *-āgi,* and *sinima* versus *bayskōpu* respectively. These differences may be accounted for historically in a variety of ways involving considerations such as regular sound change, borrowing, or analogical change. But the fact remains that such comparisons do not point to any differences in structure between the two caste dialects compared. The dialects have the same grammatical units, but in different phonological shapes. If we use the term MORPHOPHONEMICS to refer to the part of linguistic description which accounts for the phonological shapes of grammatical elements, then we may say that the type of description of caste dialects which has been illustrated above is altogether a matter of MORPHOPHONEMIC COMPARISON.

Some publications, to be sure, have also pointed out that one dialect has a different inventory of basic elements from that of another. Under phonology, for instance, it can be stated that the difference between Kanarese Brahmin *hālu,* Non-Brahmin *ālu* 'milk' reflects the fact that the Brahmin dialect has an /h/ phoneme while the Non-Brahmin dialect does not; furthermore, the Brahmin phonemes /f z š/ are also lacking in the Non-Brahmin dialect. Under the heading of grammar, however, it becomes harder to find reports of structural differences. And under the lexical heading, we again find only scant report of differences deeper than those of the morphophonemic level.

The suggestion which I would like to make is that caste dialects may differ not only in various ways that are phonologically definable, but also in important ways which are reflected in differences of grammar and vocabulary which basically derive from different semantic structures. That is, caste dialects, like separate languages (but probably to a lesser degree), may reflect different ways of classifying nonlinguistic phenomena, be they subjective or objective.

The scarcity of data on these differences probably results from several factors. For one thing, semantic differences are less obvious to the investigator than are the other types of difference which have been mentioned. In addition, semantic structure has only recently become a favored area of research for descriptive linguists. Even so, the published data on Indian social dialects provide adequate evidence that difference in semantic structures is in fact present. The following are illustrative of the data to be found:

(1) In the Tamil of the Iyengar (Brahmin) and Mudaliyar (Non-Brahmin) castes, as reported by Ramanujan (1968), the semantic area of male affinal kin is subdivided in two different ways:

	Brahmin	Non-Brahmin
son-in-law younger sister's husband	*maaple*	*marumahā*
elder sister's husband wife's brother	*attimbeer* *maccinā*	*maccā*

This particular semantic difference is, of course, correlated with differences in marriage practices.

(2) The same caste dialects of Tamil also show different classifications in the semantic area of food and water. Thus we find the following:

	Brahmin	Non-Brahmin
holy water	*perumaal tiirtõ*	*tiirtõ*
drinking water	*tiirtõ*	*taṇṇi*
water in general	*jalõ*	
nondrinkable water	*taṇṇi*	

Note here that the fact that *tiirtõ* means 'drinking water' to Brahmins and 'holy water' to Non-Brahmins means only that the two dialects overlap in their morphophonemic actualizations. The more important fact is that the Brahmin dialect uses *tiirtõ* in making a four-way distinction, while the Non-Brahmin dialect uses it in a two-way distinction.

(3) Still in the Iyengar and Mudaliyar dialects of Tamil, Brahmin usage shows connotational distinctions of meaning between certain terms which are used interchangeably in the Non-Brahmin dialect. Thus:

	Brahmin	Non-Brahmin
food (neutral)	*saadõ*	*sooru* 'food' (~ *saadõ* as free variant)
food (pejorative)	*sooru*	
eat (neutral)	*saapḍu*	*tinnu* 'eat' (~ *saapḍu* as free variant)
eat (pejorative)	*tinnu*	

(4) In the Kanarese of Dharwar, Brahmins address mother and elder sister with the same forms, while Non-Brahmins (Lingayats) make a distinction. There is a similar pattern in addressing father and elder brother.[4]

(5) Also in Dharwar, Brahmins use a single morpheme *-u* of general purpose address; Lingayats distinguish *-apa,* used to men, from *-be,* used to women; and untouchables add special elements for addressing a son-in-law and for addressing affinal kin.

(6) Again in Dharwar, Brahmins and Lingayats distinguish two cases of the noun which can be called accusative and dative, but the Untouchable dialect shows merger of the two cases into one.

(7) According to Ramaswami Aiyar (1932a), the Brahmin dialect of Tulu has a single third person honorific pronoun *ārï,* where the Non-Brahmin dialect retains a distinction (paralleled elsewhere in both dialects) between *ārï* 'he (honorific) there', and *mērï* 'he (honorific) here' (p. 903).

(8) In Brahmin Tulu, there are distinctions of gender, number, and person in negative tenses of the verb; Non-Brahmin Tulu lacks these distinctions in negative forms (ibid., p. 905).

Such differences in semantic structure may be supposed to have counterparts in other structures. It seems possible, in spite of the scarcity of data, to suggest that semantic differences between caste dialects may reflect differences in cognitive orientation from one caste to another.[5] Thus it has been suggested by various scholars that Brahmins are more concerned than other castes with verbalization, or with hierarchical classification of phenomena, or with differentiation as opposed to generalization of experience. Such hypotheses as these might derive support from the kind of data presented above. What is needed, then, is a 'social dialectology' which will apply a structural approach not only to linguistic form (Weinreich 1954), but also to meaning. If field workers will give greater attention to semantic structures, and if more data on the subject are made available, then it may be possible to fit semantic diversity into a larger understanding of how caste functions in India, and of how social stratification functions throughout the world.

NOTES

1. Material from this paper was presented at the Conference on Social Structure and Social Change in India, held at the University of Chicago in 1965. I am indebted to Punya Sloka Ray for helpful comment.

2. Bernstein (1964:66). Studies with similar aims and results, but with less careful methodology, are Schatzman and Strauss (1955) and Barth (1961).

3. Paul Friedrich (personal communication) suggests that a four-way division of Malayalam social dialects exists in Kerala, between Brahmins, Nayars, other touchable castes, and Untouchables.

4. Examples in (4), (5), and (6) are from McCormack (1960). It is McCormack's data that elicited the comment by Friedrich (1961:167) that 'the comparative componential analysis of the kinship terms in two contiguous caste dialects is perhaps of greater theoretical significance than the relatively banal issue of language as "an index of social status" '. However, such comparative componential analyses from caste dialects remain to be worked out. Shanmugam Pillai (1965a) compares kin terms from 13 castes in a Tamil community, but his interest is in the terms peculiar to single castes, and he does not give the complete data which would permit a semantic analysis.

5. Cf. the comment by Friedrich (1961:164) that "conservatism in phonemics and grammar . . . might be the linguistic aspect of the deeply internalized values of caste status among the Brahmins."

5

Complex Verb Forms in Colloquial Tamil

WITH
JACQUELINE LINDENFELD

The difference between literary Tamil and colloquial Tamil has been well characterized by Matthews (1942:992) in the following passage:

> It is a common experience for the foreigner learning Tamil to discover to his dismay that after months of study with grammar and reader and munshi he is able to understand scarcely anything of the language spoken around him. In the villages and the fields, in the bazaars and on the highroads he hears a language spoken which he finds it hard to believe is the language of his study.

The difficulty which colloquial Tamil presents to the student is aggravated by the fact that most published materials on Tamil deal primarily with the literary variety; this is true of the standard reference grammar of Arden (1942), as well as the textbook by Jothimutthu (1956). The prestige of the literary variety is so great that educated Tamilians have been known to persuade themselves that literary Tamil is their everyday spoken language; this delusion has in some cases been taken as fact by foreign linguists, resulting in alleged descriptions of colloquial Tamil which in fact apply only to very formal styles of speech (cf. Firth 1934, Fowler 1954, Kuno 1958).

To be sure, some information on colloquial Tamil has been published in works of Vinson (1895), Bloch (1910), Matthews (1942), Jothimutthu (1956), and K. Kanapathi Pillai (1958). It is only more recently, however, that more systematic treatments have become available, from the hands of Fairbanks (1957), Shanmugam Pillai (1960, 1962), Zvelebil (1959, 1960a, b, 1961, 1963a, b, c) and Andronov (1959). The present paper is an attempt to add to our understanding of colloquial Tamil by describing a part of the structure heretofore so neglected as to lack an accepted label. The label here proposed is 'Complex verb forms'.

The finite affirmative verb forms of literary Tamil have been described in structural terms by Lisker (1951); as he states, they consist of 'stem + tense marker + personal ending'. We may regard imperative forms as a special subclass of this group, distinguished by the absence of any overt tense-marker. Among the most striking features of colloquial Tamil, however, are verb forms containing additional elements of reflexive, completive, progressive, and perfective function: it is these forms which are here referred to as complex. They correspond to periphrastic expressions in literary Tamil, referred to briefly in scattered sections of Arden's grammar: 'A reflexive meaning is given by adding the verb *koḷ* to the Verbal Participle of another Verb. . . . The Verbal Participle with *koḷ* is also used to express a continuous action. . . . Occasionally *koḷ* appears to be used merely as an expletive, without modifying the meaning of the verb to which it is added' (p. 236). 'A Perfect Tense, a Pluperfect Tense, and a Future Perfect Tense are formed by prefixing the Verbal Participle of any Verb to the Present, Past and Future Tenses of *iru* "be" ' (p. 267). 'The verbs *viḍu* "leave" and *pōḍu* "put", when added to the Verbal Participles of other Verbs, intensify the meaning' (p. 282). It is the intention of this paper to show the development of these constructions in one dialect of colloquial Tamil. (Non-finite and negative verb forms show similar constructions, but their description is reserved for later publication.)

The dialect described here is that of Mrs. Shrimathy Rajangam, an educated member of the Ayyangar Brahmin community and a native of the city of Madras. Much of the data collected from this informant is confirmed by data from other Brahmin Tamilians; special thanks for such confirmation are due to Professor A. K. Ramanujan of the University of Chicago.[1] Partial data on Tamil dialects of other communities and other areas suggest that the complex verb forms of different dialects differ mainly in morphophonemics: i.e., the same morphemes are used in the same combinations, but with different phonemic realizations. The phonemic notation used for Mrs. Rajangam's speech involves the following consonant symbols: voiceless occlusives /p t ṭ c k/, voiced occlusives /b d ḍ j g/, nasals /m n ṇ/, sibilants /s š/, laterals /l ḷ/, vibrant /r/, glides /v r̤ y/, and laryngeal /h/. The vowels are short /i e a o u/, long /ī ē ā ō ū/, and nasalized /ẽ ã õ/. The phoneme /u/ has allophones [ʊ] and [ï]; there is occasional contrast between short unrounded [ï] and short rounded [u], but the latter can be accounted for by a low-level phonological rule, as resulting from /u/ in certain environments and from /ū/ in others.

The style used here for the description of complex verb forms is that of generative grammar, as presented, for example, by Bach (1964). Care is taken, however, to make the description as clear as possible by providing explanations and examples for each rule. The tactical aspects of the data are accounted for principally in terms of phrase-structure rules, plus a few transformational rules. (It may be noted that negative and non-finite verb forms would require a more complex transformational description.) The output of the tactical rules is subjected to phonological transformational rules and phonological rewriting rules; the final output consists of phonemically transcribed paradigms of colloquial Tamil finite affirmative verb forms, both simple and complex.

Phrase Structure Rules

1. #V[erb] F[orm] # → # V[erbal] Nuc[leus] + Tense + Pers[on] (+ Imp[erative])#

Brackets are used here to enclose those parts of terms which will be omitted in later abbreviated reference. Parentheses are used to enclose optional elements. Thus the rule indicates that the notion of the verb form is to be understood as involving a verbal nucleus, followed by markers of tense and person, optionally followed by an Imperative element. This 'Imp', however, is a 'dummy' symbol, in that it will not itself be rewritten by subsequent rules; its presence will trigger the operation of Transformational Rules 15–16, which produce Imperative forms. The symbol # indicates the boundaries of the verb form; certain subsequent rules operate in the environment of such an adjacent boundary.

2. VNuc → V[erb] (+ Refl[exive]) (+ Com[pletive]) (+Prog[ressive]) (+ Perf[ective])

This rule indicates that a verbal nucleus may consist of a verb, optionally followed by from one to four elements which create Reflexive, Completive, Progressive, and Perfective verb forms. Reflexive forms refer to action upon or for oneself; e.g., *vārikkarẽ* 'I comb my hair' as against *vārrẽ* 'I comb (someone else's) hair', *kuḍuttukkarã* 'he gives (for his own benefit)' as against *kuḍukkarã* 'he gives'. Completive verb forms have a meaning of finality or thoroughness which is frequently expressed in English by adverbs, e.g. *kuḍuttūḍrã* 'he gives it AWAY', *pāttūḍrã* 'he looks it OVER'. Progressive forms refer to ongoing action, e.g. *kuḍuttiṇḍrukkã* 'he is giving (now)' as against *kuḍukkarã* 'he gives (habitually)'. Perfective verb forms, like those traditionally so named in English grammar, refer to actions with effects persisting to the present, e.g. *kuḍuttirukkã* 'he has given'. There is no Perfective Imperative; this possibility is eliminated by Transformational Rules 15–16. Examples of all combinations of elements in the Verbal Nucleus can be seen in the illustrative paradigms at the end of this paper. The maximum combination, V + Refl + Com + Prog + Perf, is exemplified by *kuḍuttunūṭṭirundirukkã* 'he has been giving it away for himself'.[2]

3. V → V_1, V_2, V_3

Commas are used here to separate items between which a choice must be made. This rule thus divides verbs into three classes, permitting assignment of suffix-allomorphs according to Phonological Rules such as numbers 30 and 31. This classification of verbs is adapted from the one formulated by Lisker for literary Tamil.

4. V_1 → *kuḍuX* 'give', *sei* 'do', *kēḷX* 'ask', *aṟu* 'weep', etc.

This rule and the two following provide examples of the three classes of verbs. In order for this description to actually generate all finite affirmative verb forms of colloquial Tamil, it would, of course, be necessary to provide a complete lexicon in which all verbs were given their class assignment. The symbol *X*, appearing at the end of some verbs in Classes 1 and 2, has morphophonemic value; it is rewritten with various values by Rules 35–38. (The use of this symbol is also adapted from Lisker.)

5. V_2 → *iruX* 'be', *naḍaX* 'walk', *eri* 'throw', *vuṟu* 'fall', etc.

6. V_3 → *paṇṇ* 'make', *tūng* 'sleep', *āḍ* 'dance', *pō* 'go', etc.

Verbs cited with basic final consonant are pronounced in isolation with final /u/, by Phonological Rule 43: thus *paṇṇu* 'make', etc.

7. Refl → *d* + *kk*

The element *d* may be identified with *d* 'Past tense' (Rule 11), since it is subject to the same phonological transformations; however, no past meaning is associated with it in this rule. The element *kk* occurs only after sequences of Verb + *d,* which are equivalent to the non-finite constructions referred to in Arden's grammar as 'Verbal Participles', and elsewhere as 'Gerunds'. The element *kk* occurs unchanged in forms like *paṇṇikkarā̃* 'he makes for himself', *paṇṇikkō̃* 'it will make for itself'; its other allomorphs are described by Rules 20–24. It corresponds to the literary Tamil verb *koḷ* 'take', which is not used in the spoken language.

8. Com → *d* + *ūḍ*

The element *ūḍ* appears in this shape in forms like *kuḍuttūḍu* 'give it away!'; its other allomorphs are described in Rules 25–26. It is historically related to literary *viḍu,* colloquial *vuḍu* 'leave' (transitive). It would be misleading, however, to describe a completive construction, Verb + Past + *ūḍ,* as a sequence of Gerund + *vuḍu* 'leave'; the latter sequence might have other interpolated words, and would have to be accounted for as an example of embedding.

9. Prog → *d* + *kk* + *d* + *iruX*

An example is *kuḍuttiṇḍiru* 'be giving it!' (see Phonological Rule 22 for the development of *kk*). The element *iruX* is identifiable with the verb *iruX* 'be', since it is involved in the same phonological transformations (cf. Rule 27). The sequence *d* + *kk*, occurring here, is deleted under certain circumstances by Transformational Rules 18 and 19. Furthermore, the relative order of Prog and Com is reversed under certain circumstances, as provided by Transformational Rule 17.

10. Perf → *d* + *iruX*

An example is *kuḍuttirukkā̃* 'he has given'. Note that the combination of Refl + Perf will yield *d* + *kk* + *d* + *iruX,* which is identical with the rewriting of the Progressive marker. This results in ambiguous forms like *kuḍuttiṇḍirukkā̃,* which may mean either 'he is giving'

(Prog) or 'he has given for himself' (Refl + Perf). Still further ambiguity results from Transformational Rule 18, q.v.

11. $$\text{Tense} \rightarrow \left\{\begin{array}{ll} \textit{ar} & \text{'Present'} \\ \textit{d} & \text{'Past'} \\ \textit{v} & \text{'Future'} \end{array}\right\}$$

The braces here (like the commas in Rule 3) set off elements between which a choice must be made. The tense here glossed as 'Present', following traditional terminology, has a range of meaning like that of the English 'Present' tense; usually it indicates habitual action. The allomorphy of these tense markers is described in Rules 29–32. Examples of tense forms (from *naḍaX* 'walk') are *naḍakkarã* 'he walks', *naḍandã* 'he walked', *naḍappã* 'he will walk'.

12. $$\text{Pers} \rightarrow \left\{\begin{array}{l} \text{Non-Neut[er]} \\ \text{Neut[er]} \end{array}\right\}$$

Distinction between Neuter and other categories of Person simplifies the Phonological Transformation Rules (23, 25–26, 29).

13. $$\text{Non-Neut} \rightarrow \left\{\begin{array}{l} \textit{an} \text{ 'I'} \\ \textit{am} \text{ 'we'} \\ \textit{e} \text{ 'you' } (+\textit{ngaḷ} \text{ 'plural'}) \\ \textit{ān} \text{ 'he'} \\ \textit{āḷ} \text{ 'she'} \\ \textit{ar} \text{ 'he/she (polite)'} \\ \textit{āḷ} \text{ 'they (human)'} \end{array}\right\}$$

Zvelebil (1963a:116) gives a set of colloquial endings *-ẽ, -õ* etc. which appear different from those given above, chiefly because he is only considering utterance-final pronunciations. The basic forms presented here, however, are those occurring in Interrogative forms, which are not accounted for by Zvelebil; the utterance-final shapes are produced by Phonological Rules 44–49. Compare *naḍakkaranā* 'do I walk?' with *naḍakkarẽ* 'I walk', *naḍakkaramā* 'do we walk?' with *naḍakkarõ* 'we walk', etc.

Note that the 'she' and 'they' forms are homophonous *(āḷ)*; they are differentiated here, however, because of the need to differentiate them in the grammar of Tamil as a whole.

14. Neut → *ad* (+ *ngaḷ* 'Plural')

The varying shapes of *ad* are described by Rules 32–34. The addition of *ngaḷ* to form a Neuter Plural form is optional and relatively rare; thus the Plural form *naḍakkardungo* 'they (e.g. animals) walk' can be replaced by simple *naḍakkardu* 'it walks, they (neut.) walk'.

Transformational Rules

The following obligatory rules operate on the derivational trees produced by the phrase-structure rules, bringing about deletions, permutations, and replacements of portions of those trees.

15. VNuc + Tense + *e* 'you sg.' (+ *ngaḷ* 'Plural') + Imp ⇒ VNuc (+ *ngaḷ*)

Condition: VNuc does not contain Perf.

This rule produces 2nd person Imperative forms by deletion of the markers for tense and person; the result is an unsuffixed verb nucleus in the singular, or a verbal nucleus plus *ngaḷ* in the plural. Thus a string generated by the phrase structure rules WITHOUT the 'Imp' element might lead to *kuḍukkare* 'you give', *kuḍukkarengo* 'you pl. give'; but the same string with the 'Imp' would yield *kuḍu* 'give!', *kuḍungo* 'give (pl.)!' The condition that VNuc must not contain the Perfective element corresponds to the fact that there are no Perfective Imperative forms, although Reflexive, Completive, and Progressive forms do have Imperatives.

16. VNuc + Tense + Pers + Imp ⇒ VNuc + *aṭṭam*

Conditions: Pers does not contain *e* 'you'; VNuc does not contain Perf.

This rule produces Imperative forms which apply to all persons except 2nd person: cf. non-Imperative *kuḍukkarã* 'he gives' with Imperative *kuḍukkaṭṭõ* 'let him give'. The non-2nd person Imperative forms usually refer to 3rd person (singular or plural) when used alone, but may refer to 1st person when followed by Interrogative *ā*, as in *kuḍukkaṭṭamā* 'may I give?'[3]

17. Refl + Com + Prog + Tense ⇒ Refl + Prog + Com + Tense

This rule reverses the order of the Completive and Progressive markers, but only when they occur after the Reflexive element and without the Perfective one. Thus:

V + Refl + Com + Prog
→ V + *d* + *kk* + Com + Prog (Rule 7)
→ V + *d* + *kk* + *d* + *ūḍ* + Prog (Rule 8)

→ V + *d* + *kk* + *d* + *ūḍ* + *d* + *kk* + *d* + *iruX* (Rule 9)
⇒ V + *d* + *kk* + *d* + *kk* + *d* + *iruX* + *d* + *ūḍ*

The string thus resulting is then subject to the operation of Transformational Rule 18, which deletes one *d* + *kk* sequence, resulting in:

V + *d* + *kk* + *d* + *iruX* + *d* + *ūḍ*

This derivation leads to forms like *kuḍuttiṇḍirundūḍrā* 'he is giving it away for himself'.

18. *d* + *kk* + *d* + *kk* ⇒ *d* + *kk*

This rule operates to delete one of the pair of *d* + *kk* sequences which result when Refl *(d + kk)* is immediately followed by Prog *(d + kk + d + iruX)*. It has the effect of adding additional ambiguity to that described under Rule 10. Thus:

(a) V + Prog
→ V + *d* + *kk* + *d* + *iruX* (Rule 9)

(b) V + Refl + Perf
→ V + *d* + *kk* + Perf (Rule 7)
→ V + *d* + *kk* + *d* + *iruX* (Rule 10)

(c) V + Refl + Prog
→ V + *d* + *kk* + Prog (Rule 7)
→ V + *d* + *kk* + *d* + *kk* + *d* + *iruX* (Rule 9)
⇒ V + *d* + *kk* + *d* + *iruX*

All three of these derivations lead to forms like *kuḍuttiṇḍirukkā*, which may thus mean 'he is giving', 'he has given for himself', or 'he is giving for himself'.

19. *d* + *ūḍ* + *d* + *kk* ⇒ *d* + *ūḍ*

This rule deletes the *d* + *kk* part of the Progressive element when it immediately follows the Completive element. Thus:

(a) V + Com + Prog + Perf
→ V + *d* + *ūḍ* + Prog + Perf (Rule 8)
→ V + *d* + *ūḍ* + *d* + *kk* + *d* + *iruX* + Perf (Rule 9)
→ V + *d* + *ūḍ* + *d* + *kk* + *d* + *iruX* + *d* + *iruX* (Rule 10)
⇒ V + *d* + *ūḍ* + *d* + *iruX* + *d* + *iruX*

This derivation leads to forms like *kuḍuttūṭṭirundirukkā* 'he has been giving it away'.

This same deletion rule results in ambiguous forms in the following case:

(b) V + Com + Perf
→ V + *d* + *ūḍ* + Perf (Rule 8)
→ V + *d* + *ūḍ* + *d* + *iruX* (Rule 10)

(c) V + Com + Prog
→ V + *d* + *ūḍ* + Prog (Rule 8)
→ V + *d* + *ūḍ* + *d* + *kk* + *d* + *iruX* (Rule 9)
⇒ V + *d* + *ūḍ* + *d* + *iruX*

Both of these derivations lead to forms like *kuḍuttūṭṭirukkā̃,* which may thus mean either 'he has given it away' or 'he is giving it away'.

Phonological Transformations

The following rules assign phonological shapes to morphemes which have been introduced in the preceding rules. These rules are transformational in nature, in that they operate on derivational trees; however, unlike the preceding Transformational Rules, those of this group are to be applied in the order given.

20. *kk* + *d* ⇒ *n* in env[ironment] ___ *ūḍ*

This rule indicates that the sequence of *kk* (occurring in the Reflexive and Progressive elements) plus *d,* when the latter forms part of the Completive marker, is replaced by *n*. Examples are *naḍandunūḍrā̃* 'he walks completely for himself', *paṇṇinūḍrā̃* 'he makes completely for himself'.

21. *kk* ⇒ *ṇ* in env $\left\{ \begin{array}{l} V_3 + d \_\_\_ \\ d \_\_\_ d + \text{Pers} \end{array} \right\}$

The element *kk* takes the form *ṇ* after Class 3 verbs, or when immediately followed by the sequence of Past tense and Person marker; e.g. *paṇṇinḍā̃* 'he made for himself', *naḍanduṇḍā̃* 'he walked for himself'. The fact that the rules of this section are ordered implies that this rule operates in cases OTHER than those covered by the previous rule; hence it does not operate when *kk* is in the environment before *d* + *ūḍ*.

22. *kk* ⇒ *iṇ* in env *d* ___ *d* + *iruX*

The element *kk* takes the form *iṇ* after verbs of Classes 1 and 2, when followed by *iruX*: thus *kuḍuttiṇḍirukkā̃* 'he is giving', *naḍandiṇḍirukkā̃* 'he is walking'.

23. *kk* + *v* ⇒ $\left\{ \begin{array}{c} kkuv \\ pp \end{array} \right\}$ in env ___ NonNeut

This option in the combination of *kk* with *v* 'Future' produces pairs like *paṇṇikkuvā̃* or *paṇṇippā̃,* both meaning 'he will make for himself'.

24. *kk* ⇒ *kko* in env ___ #

Since the symbol # indicates the end of the verb form, this rule accounts for 2nd person singular Imperative forms like *paṇṇikko* 'make for yourself!', where no overt personal element follows the Reflexive marker.

Where Rules 20–24 do not operate, the element *kk* retains its basic form, e.g. in *paṇṇikkarā̃* 'he makes for himself', *paṇṇikkō̃* 'it will make for itself', *paṇṇikkungo* 'make for yourselves!'.

25. *d* + *ūḍ* + *d* + ⇒ *īr* in env V_3 ___ Neut

This rule operates in Past Neuter Completive forms of Class 3 verbs, resulting in forms like *paṇṇīrtu* 'it made completely'.

25a. *d* + *ūḍ* ⇒ *īḍ* in env V_3 ___

This rule operates in other Completive forms of Class 3 verbs, producing forms like *paṇṇīḍrā̃* 'he makes completely', *paṇṇīṭṭā̃* 'he made completely', *paṇṇīḍu* 'make completely!'.

26. *ūḍ* + *d* ⇒ *ūr* in env ___ Neut

This rule operates in Past Neuter Completive forms of Class 1 and 2 verbs, resulting in forms like *naḍandūrtu* 'it walked completely'.

Where Rules 25 and 26 do not operate, the element *ūḍ* retains its basic form, e.g. in *naḍandūḍu* 'walk completely!', *naḍandunūḍu* 'walk completely for yourself!', *paṇṇinūḍu* 'make completely for yourself!'.[4]

27. *ar* ⇒ Ø in env *iruX* ___

This rule indicates that the Present tense marker has a zero form in the environment after *iruX* 'be' (including its appearance as part of the Progressive and Perfective elements). Thus the present tense of this verb has forms like *iruX* + Ø + *īn* → *irukkā̃* 'he is' (by Phonological Rules 35 and 48). After other verbs, the Present marker retains its form *ar,* as in *aṛarā̃* 'he weeps', *eriyarā̃* 'he throws', *paṇrā̃* 'he makes', *naḍakkarā̃* 'he walks'.

28. $d + adu \Rightarrow \left\{\begin{array}{l} ccu \\ cci \end{array}\right\}$ in env $\left\{\begin{array}{l} p\tilde{o} \text{ 'go'} \\ \tilde{a} \text{ 'become'} \end{array}\right\}$ ___

This rule produces Past Neuter forms from two irregular verbs: *pōccu* (more formal) or *pōcci* (less formal) 'it goes', etc.

29. *d* ⇒ *in* in env V_3 ___ NonNeut

Examples are *paṇṇinā̃* 'he made', *tūnginā̃* 'he slept', *pōnā̃* 'he went'.

30. *d* ⇒ *i* in env V_3 ____

This rule operates in most environments after V_3 except before a NonNeuter suffix; i.e., *i* occurs before the Neuter suffix and in the 'Gerund', where no suffix of person follows. Examples are *paṇṇittu* 'it made', *paṇṇikkarã* 'he makes for himself', *paṇṇiṇḍirukkã* 'he is making it', *paṇṇiirukkã* 'he has made it'.

31. *d* ⇒ *nd* in env V_2 ____

Examples are *naḍandã* 'he walked', *irundã* 'he was', *vuṟundã* 'he fell'.

Where rules 20, 25–26, and 29–31 do not operate, viz. after V_1, the Past marker retains its form *d*, as in *seidã* 'he did', *aṟuã* 'he wept'. By Rule 36, the morphophoneme *X* combines with *d* to form *tt* in examples like *kuḍuttã* 'he gave' (from *kuḍuX* 'give'.) By Rule 41, this *tt* is replaced after /i/ by *cc*: thus, from *paḍiX* 'study', *paḍiccã* 'he studied'.

32. *v* + *ad* + *ngaḷ* ⇒ *ungaḷ*

This rule produces Future forms with Neuter Plural subjects, e.g. *naḍakkungo* 'they (neut.) will walk'.

32a. *v* + *ad* ⇒ *om*

This Future Neuter ending appears as *om* before Interrogative *ā*, as in *paṇṇomā* 'will it make?', but as *õ* (by Rule 46) when in word-final position, as in *paṇṇõ* 'it will make'. Some speakers have phonemic contrast between /õ/ and /ũ/; in their dialects, the Future Neuter ending has the forms *um* and *ũ*, the latter contrasting with the final vowel of such forms as *paṇṇaṭṭõ* 'let him make'.

Where Rules 23 and 32–32a do not operate, the Future marker preserves the form *v*, e.g. in *paṇṇuvã* 'he will make', *seivã* 'he will do', *vuṟuvã* 'he will fall'. The morphophoneme *X* combines with *v* (by Rule 37) to form *pp*, as in *naḍappã* 'he will walk' (from *naḍaX* 'walk').

33. *ad* ⇒ *ud* in env *iruX* ____

This rule operates where the Present tense marker after *iruX* has been zeroed out (by Rule 27). The result is forms like *irukkudu* 'it is', *naḍandirukkudu* 'it has walked'.

34. *ad* ⇒ *tt* in env $\left\{\begin{matrix} V_3 \\ \bar{u}\d{d} \end{matrix}\right\}$ + *d* ____

The Neuter suffix takes this form in cases like *paṇṇittu* 'it made' and in Completive forms like *kuḍuttūrtu* 'it gave away' (with the operation of Rule 51).

In all other environments than those specified in Rules 28 and 32–34, the Neuter suffix retains the form *ad,* e.g. in *pākkardu* 'it sees', *naḍakkardu* 'it walks', *paṉradu* 'it makes', *naḍandūḍradu* 'it walks completely', *naḍandukkardu* 'it walks for itself'.

Phonological Rules

The following ordered rules apply to sequences of morphophonemes and phonemes generated by the previous rules, regardless of grammatical considerations. This section is incomplete, in that some rules of rare application are omitted; it is, however, adequate to generate the paradigms of most verbs.

35. *X* → *kk* in env ____ /V|owel]/

The morphophoneme *X,* already noted as occurring finally in many verbs of Classes 1 and 2, is replaced by *kk* before vowels (here symbolized by /V/); e.g., from *naḍaX* 'walk', *naḍakkarã* 'he walks', *naḍakkõ* 'it will walk', *naḍakkaṭṭõ* 'let him walk' (cf. also the non-finite 'Infinitive' *naḍakka* 'to walk'.) The symbol /V/ for 'vowel' which is used in this rule has not, of course, been defined in the rules themselves. In a more rigorous generative grammar, with forms united in terms of distinctive feature matrices, this rule might be restated to read 'in env ____ Consonantal-Nonconsonantal MINUS, Vocalic-Nonvocalic PLUS'. For greater convenience in the present description, however, 'vowel' may be interpreted as one of the units so defined in the introductory portion of this paper.

36. *X* + *d* → *tt*

This rule applies in the Past tense of Class 1 verbs, accounting for derivations like *kuḍuX* 'give' + *d* 'Past' + *ān* 'he' → *kuḍuttã* 'he gave', *kuḍuX* + *d* + *kko* 'Reflexive' → *kuḍuttukko* 'give for yourself!'

37. *X* + *v* → *pp*

This rule applies in the Future tense of Class 1 and 2 verbs, so that *kuḍuX* 'give' + *v* 'Future' + *ān* → *kuḍuppã* 'he gives', *naḍaX* 'walk' + *v* + *ān* → *naḍappã* 'he will walk'.

38. X → Ø

The morphophoneme *X* is zeroed out in environments other than those stated above; e.g., *naḍaX* 'walk' + *nd* 'Past' + *ān* → *naḍandã* 'he walked', *naḍaX* + *ngo* 'Plural' → *naḍango* 'walk (pl.)!' This rule also accounts for the zeroing of *X* in word-final position, in 2nd person singular Imperatives, e.g. *naḍaX* → *naḍa* 'walk!'

39. *d* → *ḍ* in env /ṇ/ ____

Examples involve the Past tense marker *d,* as in *naḍaX* 'walk' + *nd* 'Past' + *iṇ* 'Reflexive' + *d* 'Past' + *iruX* 'be' → *naḍandiṇḍiru* 'be walking!'

40. *ḍ* + *d* → *ṭṭ*

Examples again involve the Past tense marker, e.g. *naḍaX* 'walk' + *nd* 'Past' + *ūḍ* 'Completive' + *d* 'Past' + *ān* 'he' → *naḍandūṭṭã* 'he walked completely'.

41. *tt* → *cc* in env $/V_f + /$ ____

The symbol $/V_f/$ here represents 'front vowels', specifically /i/ and /e/. The plus after the symbol indicates that the rule operates only when *tt* is preceded by a morpheme boundary. Examples are *paḍiX* 'study' + *d* 'Past' + *ān* 'he' → **paḍi+ttã* → *paḍiccã* 'he studied', *sameX* 'cook' + *d* + *ān* → **same+ttã* → *sameccã* 'he cooked'.

42. *cc* → *cci* in env $\_\_\_\_ \left\{ \begin{array}{l} /\text{C[onsonant]}/ \\ \# \end{array} \right\}$

When applied after Rule 41, this rule accounts for developments such as *paḍiX* 'study' + *d* 'Past' → **paḍicc* → *paḍicci.* This sequence, existing alone as the non-finite gerund 'having studied', occurs along with Reflexive *kk* in such examples as *paḍiccikko* 'study for yourself!'

43. $/C_1/ \rightarrow /C_1u/$ in env $\_\_\_\_ \left\{ \begin{array}{c} /C_2/ \\ \# \end{array} \right\}$

The symbol $/C_1/$ stands for any consonant except /m n ḷ r/; $/C_2/$ stands for any consonant not identical with $/C_1/$. This rule operates in all cases not covered by preceding rules, eliminating many consonantal syllable-codas by the introduction of a 'euphonic' /u/. Thus *paṇṇ* 'make' + *v* 'Future' + *ān* 'he' → *paṇṇuvã* 'he will make', *naḍaX* 'walk' + *nd* 'Past' + *kko* 'Reflexive' → *naḍandukko* 'walk for yourself!'; *naḍaX* + *nd* + *kk* 'Reflexive' + *v* 'Future' + *ān* 'he' → *naḍandukkuvã* 'he will walk for himself'.

44. *am* → *õ* in env ____ #

E.g., *kuḍuX* 'give' + *aṭṭam* 'non-2nd pers. Imperative' → *kuḍuk-*

kaṭṭõ 'let him give', *kuḍuX* + *ar* 'Present' + *am* 'we' → *kuḍukkarõ* 'we give'. The rule also operates in noun forms: *maram* 'tree' → *marõ* before #.

45. *an* → *ẽ* in env ___ #

E.g., *kuḍuX* 'give' + *ar* 'Present' + *an* 'I' → *kuḍukkarẽ* 'I give'. The rule also operates in other than verb forms: *avan* 'he' → *avẽ* before #.

46. *om* → *õ* in env ___ #

E.g., *paṇṇ* 'do' + *v* 'Future' + *adu* 'Neuter' → **paṇṇom* → *paṇṇõ* 'it will do'.

47. *aḷ* → *o* in env ___ #

E.g., *kuḍuX* 'give' + *ar* 'Present' + *engaḷ* 'you pl.' → *kuḍukka-rengo* 'you pl. give'.

48. *ān* → *ā in* env ___ #

E.g., *kuḍuX* 'give' + *ar* 'Present' + *ān* 'he' → *kuḍukkarā* 'he gives'.

49. *āḷ* → *ā* in env ___ #

E.g., *kuḍuX* + *ar* + *āḷ* 'she' or 'they' → *kuḍukkarā* 'she gives, they give'.

50. *a* → in env $\left\{\begin{array}{l} /r/\_\_\_/C_a/ \\ /C_a/\_\_\_/r/ \end{array}\right\}$

The symbol $/C_a/$ stands for any apical consonant, i.e. /t d n l r ṭ ḍ ṇ ḷ/. The rule indicates that the vowel *a* is lost between any of these consonants and /r/. E.g., *naḍaX* 'walk' + *ar* 'Present' + *ad* 'Neuter' → **naḍakkaradu* → *naḍakkardu* 'it walks'; *naḍaX* + *nd* 'Past' + *ūḍ* 'Completive' + *ar* + *ān* 'he' → **naḍandūḍarā* → *naḍandūḍrā* 'he walks completely'.

51. $C_1C_1 \rightarrow C_1$ in env $\left\{\begin{array}{l} \_\_\_\ C \\ C\ \_\_\_ \end{array}\right\}$

The symbolization 'C_1C_1' indicates a sequence of identical consonants. This rule operates in many cases after a vowel *a* has been dropped by the preceding rule: e.g., *paṇṇ* 'make' + *ar* 'Present' + *ān* 'he' → **paṇṇarā* → **paṇṇrā* → *paṇrā* 'he makes'; *var* 'come' + *aṭṭam* 'non-2nd pers. Imperative' → **varaṭṭõ* → **varṭṭõ* → *varṭõ* 'let him come.'

Appendix: Sample Paradigms

V_1 + Tense + Pers (V_1 has final *X*)

Present:	1 sg.	*kuḍukkarẽ* 'I give'
	1 pl.	*kuḍukkarõ*
	2 sg.	*kuḍukkare*
	2 pl.	*kuḍukkarengo*
	3 m.	*kuḍukkarã*
	3 f.	*kuḍukkarā*
	3 pol.	*kuḍukkarar*
	3 pl.	*kuḍukkarā*
	3 n.	*kuḍukkardu*
	3 n. pl.	*kuḍukkardungo*
Past:	3 m.	*kuḍuttã* 'he gave'
	3 n.	*kuḍuttadu*
Future:	3 m.	*kuḍuppã* 'he will give'
	3 n.	*kuḍukkõ*
Imperative:	2 sg.	*kuḍu* 'give!'
	2 pl.	*kuḍungo*
	1–3.	*kuḍukkaṭṭõ*

V_1 + Tense + Pers (V_1 does not have final *X*)

Present:	3 m.	*ar̤arã* 'he weeps'
	3 n.	*ar̤ardu*
Past:	3 m.	*ar̤udã* 'he wept'
	3 n.	*ar̤udadu*
Future:	3 m.	*ar̤uvã* 'he will weep'
	3 n.	*ar̤õ*
Imperative:	2 sg.	*ar̤u* 'weep!'

V_2 + Tense + Pers (V_2 has final *X*)

Present:	3 m.	*naḍakkarã* 'he walks'
	3 n.	*naḍakkardu*
Past:	3 m.	*naḍandã* 'he walked'
	3 n.	*naḍandadu*

Future:	3 m.	*naḍappã* 'he will walk'
	3 n.	*naḍakkõ*
Imperative:	2 sg.	*naḍa* 'walk!'

V_2 + Tense + Pers (V_2 does not have final *X*)

Present:	3 m.	*vur̤arã* 'he falls'
	3 n.	*vur̤ardu*
Past:	3 m.	*vur̤undã* 'he fell'
	3 n.	*vur̤undadu*
Future:	3 m.	*vur̤uvã* 'he will fall'
	3 n.	*vur̤õ*
Imperative:	2 sg.	*vur̤u* 'fall!'

V_3 + Tense + Pers

Present:	3 m.	*paṇrã* 'he makes'
	3 n.	*paṇradu*
Past:	3 m.	*paṇṇinã* 'he made'
	3 n.	*paṇṇittu*
Future:	3 m.	*paṇṇuvã* 'he will make'
	3 n.	*paṇṇõ*
Imperative:	2 sg.	*paṇṇu* 'make!'

V_1 + Refl + Tense + Pers

Present:	3 m.	*kuḍuttukkarã* 'he gives for himself'
	3 n.	*kuḍuttukkardu*
Past:	3 m.	*kuḍuttuṇḍã* 'he gave for himself'
	3 n.	*kuḍuttuṇḍadu*
Future:	3 m.	*kuḍuttukkuvã, kuḍuttuppã* 'he will give for himself'
	3 n.	*kuḍuttukkõ*
Imperative:	2 sg.	*kuḍuttukko* 'give for yourself!'

V_3 + Refl + Tense + Pers

Present:	3 m.	*paṇṇikkarã* 'he makes for himself'
	3 n.	*paṇṇikkardu*

Past:	3 m.	*paṇṇiṇḍã* 'he made for himself'
	3 n.	*paṇṇiṇḍadu*
Future:	3 m.	*paṇṇikkuvã, paṇṇippã* 'he will make for himself'
	3 n.	*paṇṇikkõ*
Imperative:	2sg.	*paṇṇikko* 'make for yourself!'

V_1 + Com + Tense + Pers

Present:	3 m.	*kuḍuttūḍrã* 'he gives away'
	3 n.	*kuḍuttūḍradu*
Past:	3 m.	*kuḍuttūṭṭã* 'he gave away'
	3 n.	*kuḍuttūrtu*
Future:	3 m.	*kuḍuttūḍuvã* 'he will give away'
	3 n.	*kuḍuttūḍõ*
Imperative:	2 sg.	*kuḍuttūḍu* 'give away!'

V_3 + Com + Tens + Pers

Present:	3 m.	*paṇṇīḍrã* 'he makes completely'
	3 n.	*paṇṇīḍradu*
Past:	3 m.	*paṇṇīṭṭã* 'he made completely'
	3 n.	*paṇṇīrtu*
Future:	3 m.	*paṇṇīḍuvã* 'he will make completely'
	3 n.	*paṇṇīḍõ*
Imperative:	2 sg.	*paṇṇīḍu* 'make completely!'

V + Prog + Tense + Pers

Present:	3 m.	*kuḍuttiṇḍirukkã* 'he is giving'
	3 n.	*kuḍuttiṇḍirukkadu*
Past:	3 m.	*kuḍuttiṇḍirundã* 'he was giving'
	3 n.	*kuḍuttiṇḍirundadu*
Future:	3 m.	*kuḍuttiṇḍiruppã* 'he will be giving'
	3 n.	*kuḍuttiṇḍirukkõ*
Imperative:	2 sg.	*kuḍuttiṇḍiru* 'be giving!'

V + Perf + Tense + Pers

Present:	3 m.	*kuḍuttirukkã* 'he has given'
	3 n.	*kupḍuttirukkadu*

Past:	3 m.	*kuḍuttirundã* 'he had given'
	3 n.	*kuḍuttirundadu*
Future:	3 m.	*kuḍuttiruppã* 'he will have given'
	3 n.	*kuḍuttirukkõ*

V + Refl + Com + Tense + Pers

Present:	3 m.	*kuḍuttunūḍrã* 'he gives away for himself'
Past:	3 m.	*kuḍuttunūṭṭã* 'he gave away for himself'
Future:	3 m.	*kuḍuttunūḍuvã* 'he will give away for himself'
Imperative:	2 sg.	*kuḍuttunūḍu* 'give away for yourself!'

V + Refl + Prog + Tense + Pers

Present:	3 m.	*kuḍuttiṇḍirukkã* 'he is giving for himself'
Past:	3 m.	*kuḍuttiṇḍirundã* 'he was giving for himself'
Future:	3 m.	*kuḍuttiṇḍiruppã* 'he will be giving for himself'
Imperative:	2 sg.	*kuḍuttiṇḍiru* 'be giving for yourself!'

V + Refl + Perf + Tense + Pers

Present:	3 m.	*kuḍuttiṇḍirukkã* 'he has given for himself'
Past:	3 m.	*kuḍuttiṇḍirundã* 'he had given for himself'
Future:	3 m.	*kuḍuttiṇḍiruppã* 'he will have given for himself'

V + Com + Prog + Tense + Pers

Present:	3 m.	*kuḍuttūṭṭirukkã* 'he is giving away'
Past:	3 m.	*kuḍuttūṭṭirundã* 'he was giving away'
Future:	3 m.	*kuḍuttūṭṭiruppã* 'he will be giving away'
Imperative:	2 sg.	*kuḍuttūṭṭiru* 'be giving away!'

V + Com + Perf + Tense + Pers

Present:	3 m.	*kuḍuttūṭṭirukkã* 'he has given away'
Past:	3 m.	*kuḍuttūṭṭirundã* 'he had given away'
Future:	3 m.	*kuḍuttūṭṭiruppã* 'he will have given away'

V + Prog + Perf + Tense + Pers

Present: 3 m. *kuḍuttiṇḍirundirukkā̃* 'he has been giving'
Past: 3 m. *kuḍuttiṇḍirundirundā̃* 'he had been giving'
Future: 3 m. *kuḍuttiṇḍirundiruppā̃* 'he will have been giving'

V + Refl + Com + Prog + Tense + Pers (⇒ V + Refl + Prog + Com . . . , Rule 17)

Present: 3 m. *kuḍuttiṇḍirundū̃ḍrā̃* 'he is giving away for himself'
Past: 3 m. *kuḍuttiṇḍirundū̃ṭṭā̃* 'he was giving away for himself'
Future: 3 m. *kuḍuttiṇḍirundū̃ḍuvā̃* 'he will be giving away for himself'
Imperative: 2 sg. *kuḍuttiṇḍirundū̃ḍu* 'be giving away for yourself!'

V + Refl + Com + Perf + Tense + Pers

Present: 3 m. *kuḍuttunū̃ṭṭirukkā̃* 'he has given away for himself'
Past: 3 m. *kuḍuttunū̃ṭṭirundā̃* 'he had given away for himself'
Future: 3 m. *kuḍuttunū̃ṭṭiruppā̃* 'he will have given away for himself'

V + Refl + Prog + Perf + Tense + Pers

Present: 3 m. *kuḍuttiṇḍirundirukkā̃* 'he has been giving for himself'
Past: 3 m. *kuḍuttiṇḍirundirundā̃* 'he had been giving for himself'
Future: 3 m. *kuḍuttiṇḍirundiruppā̃* 'he will have been giving for himself'

V + Com + Prog + Perf + Tense + Pers

Present: 3 m. *kuḍuttū̃ṭṭirundirukkā̃* 'he has been giving away'

Past: 3 m. *kuḍuttūṭṭirundirundā̃* 'he had been giving away'

Future: 3 m. *kuḍuttūṭṭirundiruppā̃* 'he will have been giving away'

V + Refl + Com + Prog + Perf + Tense + Pers

Present: 3 m. *kuḍuttunūṭṭirundirukkā̃* 'he has been giving away for himself'

Past: 3 m. *kuḍuttunūṭṭirundirundā̃* 'he had been giving away for himself'

Future: 3 m. *kuḍuttunūṭṭirundiruppā̃* 'he will have been giving away for himself.'

NOTES

1. We have also benefited from a number of analytic insights provided by Prof. Ramanujan. This paper would have been enhanced if time had permitted us to follow up more of his suggestions. Thanks are further due to Gérard Diffloth for his constructive criticism.

2. It is possible that, in a total grammar of Tamil, the verb complexes treated here would be better handled as special cases of the more general type of construction by which one verbal predication may be imbedded in another. The present description seems simpler, however, for the limited aim of our study. It should be noted that not all of the complex forms which are cited and described here are equally 'normal' or 'natural'; many of them are as unusual and clumsy as an English expression like 'it would have been being given'. We believe, however, that they are all 'grammatical' as far as our informant is concerned.

3. The non-2nd person Imperative should perhaps not be generated as part of the finite paradigm, but rather treated as a modal construction; so *kuḍuk-kaṭṭō* 'let (someone) give' would be treated like *kuḍukka vēṇō* '(someone) should give'. This alternative description is supported by the fact that the forms in *aṭṭam* occur before Interrogative *ā,* while the second person Imperatives do not.

4. Where medial vowels of Completive forms are written as *ī* and *ū,* either long or short vowels occur in pronunciation (*ū* preserving its rounding, even when shortened.) This is here treated as a subphonemic development.

6

Phonological Rules in Literary and Colloquial Kannada

It has been recognized for some time that the languages of India present several cases of the phenomenon which Ferguson (1959) has called diglossia: the co-existence of two styles of speech having a common origin but only a limited degree of mutual intelligibility, and functionally specialized in terms of a literary vs. colloquial dichotomy.[1] Such diglossia has been described for Bengali and Tamil,[2] as well as for the language under discussion in the present paper: Kannada (Kanarese), the Dravidian language of Mysore State in South India. The older reference grammars of the language are based on literary style alone; but in recent years several varieties of colloquial Kannada have been described, the most detailed treatments being my own description of Bangalore usage, Hiremath's of Dharwar, and Upadhyaya's of four more localities (Gulbarga, Bellary, Kumta, and Nanjangud).[3] However, all of these works are essentially on the model of neo-Bloomfieldian, taxonomic grammar, and there is little attempt to show the relationship of the colloquial dialects described either to the corresponding literary style or to historical origins. Thus particular interest attaches to a recent work by H. Manappa Nayak, originally written as an Indiana University dissertation, and now published (1967) under the title *Kannada, Literary and Colloquial: A study of two styles.*[4] Nayak's book not only has greater sociolinguistic sophistication than the other works cited, but even (in one brief section) promises to follow 'the technique of Transformational-Generative grammars' (p. 69).[5]

Unfortunately, Nayak's study does not live up to its promise. What it provides is, essentially, a list of surface-structure correspondences between literary and colloquial Kannada, without explanation in terms of deeper-level structures, of cross-dialectal comparison, or historical background. Like the other works I have cited, it fails to account for the following facts: (1) For the most part, literary Kannada is an archaism, a stage which the language reached some centuries ago, when it became ''frozen' by social convention. The colloquial dialects, which are spoken as everyone's first language, continued to change, while the literary style was preserved for the use of an educated minority. But the result was that modern literary Kannada represents, to a large extent, an earlier historical stage of the modern colloquial dialects. (2) As a result, the morphophonemically BASIC FORMS of the colloquial dialects are to a large extent identical with literary Kannada—just as the morphophonemically basic forms of French are much closer to Latin than the actual pronunciation of modern French.[6] (3) Similarly, the synchronic morphophonemic rules of colloquial Kannada reflect, to a large extent, the processes of historical sound change which characterize the modern colloquial dialects. All of this is to say that Nayak, in making an artificial barrier between synchrony and diachrony, has cut himself off from a historical perspective,[7] one which would make it possible to explain, not merely to classify, his data.

In the present paper I attempt to formulate some phonological rules which will have both diachronic and synchronic validity for Kannada. Lexicon, grammar, and phonological alternations peculiar to particular morphemes are not dealt with here; nor is there any attempt to account for all dialects of colloquial Kannada, since we have adequate data on relatively few. Rules will be stated in an informal way, without reference to possible distinctive-feature analyses; but the order of their application IS significant. The rules are intended to operate on Kannada morphemes in a phonological transcription which is 'morphophonemically basic' in neo-Bloomfieldian terminology, or 'systematic-phonemic' in Chomskyan terms; the output of the rules should be phonetic symbols reflecting the pronunciation of literary and colloquial Kannada.

(1) First of all, it must be specified that a large number of Sanskrit loanwords are used in Kannada, and that compounds of such elements

obey Sanskrit sandhi rules: e.g. *deva* 'god' + *ālaya* 'place' → *devālaya* 'temple'. Nayak has listed some of these as his morphophonemic rules 11–12 for both styles (p. 71) and rules 2–3 for the literary style (p. 73); the whole list may be found in, e.g., Emeneau and van Nooten (1968).

(2) Some words of Sanskrit origin, however, undergo different changes when they are used outside of Sanskrit compounds. Specifically, final *ā* regularly becomes *e*: cf. *bhāṣā* 'language', compounded as *bhāṣā-śāstra* 'linguistics', but otherwise occurring as *bhāṣe*. Feminine proper names obey this rule only for some speakers: *sītā* may or may not become *sīte*. Some loans from modern Indo-Aryan, by contrast, normally preserve final *ā*, e.g. *rajā* 'holiday'.

(3) The Sanskrit syllabic *r̥* is replaced by *ri* or *ru*, as in *r̥tu* → *ritu* ~ *rutu* 'season' (*OCK* p. 2, §1.3.2).

(4) A number of morphophonemic changes affect the consonant clusters which result when verb stems are combined with the past-tense suffix *-d* ~ *-t* (Nayak p. 70, rules 3–4; p. 73, rule 4). Many of these changes apply quite irregularly to one or two stems; e.g. *kol-* 'kill', *kon-d-a* 'he killed', but *gel-* 'win', *ged-d-a* 'he won'. A list of the major types appears in *OCK*, pp. 22–23. Similar rules apply in the other South Dravidian languages, and thus seem likely to have considerable historical depth.

(5) After *ṇ*, *d* becomes *ḍ*, e.g. in *kāṇ* 'see' + *-d* 'past': *kaṇ-ḍ-a* 'he saw' (*OCK* p. 17, §2.11.1; Nayak, p. 73, rule 21).

(6) A long vowel becomes short before two consonants, as in the example just above, and similarly in *bīḷ-* 'fall', past **bīd-d-a* → *bidda* 'he fell' (*OCK* p. 16, §2.7; Nayak p. 70, rule 5).

(7) Several other sound changes are peculiar to particular combinations of morphemes: cf. *hāvu* 'snake' with *heb-bāvu* 'big snake, i.e. python'. (More examples appear in *OCK* p. 18, §2.11.6; and in Nayak p. 71, rules 7–8, 13–15.)

(8) Many Kannada morphemes, in their basic phonological shape, end in consonants; when these are followed by pause, or by a word boundary plus consonant, the 'enunciative vowel' must be inserted: *i* after *y*, as in *nāy-* 'dog' → *nāyi*, and *u* elsewhere, as in *māḍ-* 'do' → *māḍu*. An exception involves recent loans with final resonants: *ḍazan* 'dozen', *huṣār* 'be careful!' (*OCK*, p. 13, §2.2).

(9) In the basic forms of native Kannada stems the only contrastive geminate consonants are the voiced stops and the resonants (*m n ṇ l ḷ*

v y, but not *r*); examples are *habe* 'steam' vs. *habba* 'festival', *huḷi* 'sour' vs. *baḷḷi* 'vine', *rave* 'grits' vs. *tovve* 'dhall'. Other consonants are predictably long after the first vowel of a word, except in Sanskrit loans; thus we have large numbers of words like *kappe* 'frog', *buṭṭi* 'basket', *hakki* 'bird', as compared with a few Sanskrit words like *kapi* 'monkey'. Furthermore, monosyllabic stems ending in any consonant will show gemination, as well as the added enunciative vowel, when produced in isolation: *tap-* 'wrong' → *tappu, kay-* 'hand' → *kayyi, kol-* 'kill' → *kollu*. This operates even in English loans, producing geminates unknown in native words: *bas-* 'bus' → *bassu, braṣ-* 'brush' → *braṣṣu*.

(10) In certain cases where vowels come into contact, a semivowel is inserted between them: *v* if the first vowel is *a* or *u*, and *y* if it is *e* or *i*. Examples are *magu* 'child', *maguv-ina* 'of a child'; *kuḍi* 'drink', *kuḍiy-uva* 'drinking' (*OCK* p. 17, §2.9; Nayak p. 70, rule 2).

The operation of the above rules will result in a transcription which corresponds rather closely to literary Kannada orthography, and which in fact amounts to a taxonomic-phonemic notation for the literary style. This transcription is further subject only to phonetic rules which apply to both literary and colloquial styles, and which will be given below.

Rules which now follow operate on the output of those above, and produce forms in the colloquial style. Basic reference is made to the urban colloquial standard of Bangalore (Ba.), and secondarily to Nayak's data from Shimoga (Shi.) and Hiremath's from Dharwar (Dh.)

(11) The sequences *iyV* and *eyV*, resulting from rule 10, contract to single long vowels, in a number of ways. In Shimoga, *iya* → *ē*, as in *huḍugi-aru* 'girls' → *huḍgiyaru* → *huḍgēru;* and *eya* → *ǣ*, e.g. *mane-alli* 'at home' → *maneyalli* → *manǣlli* (Nayak p. 72, rules 7–8); in Bangalore, the usual results would be *ī* and *ē* respectively (*huḍgīru, manēlli*). In both dialects, *iyu* becomes *ī*, e.g. *bari* 'write', *bari-ut(t)-āne* 'he writes' → *bariyutāne* → *barītāne*. Sequences of the type *iyV* and *eyV* are also replaced by long vowels when word-final, in both dialects: e.g., *mane* 'house', nom. *mane-u* → *maneyu* → *manē;* gen. *mane-a* → *maneya* → *manē*, homonymous with the nominative.[8]

(12) The sequences *avV* and *uvV*, also resulting from rule 11, contract to *ā* and *ū* respectively, in forms like *mara* 'tree', nom. *mara-u* → *maravu* → *marā; guru* 'preceptor', gen. *guru-a* → *guruva* → *gurū*.

(13) The most striking characteristic of the colloquial dialects is that short vowels tend to be reduced in prominence and lost when they are

not in word-initial syllables; e.g., *hancisidaru* 'they distributed' → *hancsdru*. This loss also affects word-final short vowels in certain syllabic environments: *avanige koḍu* 'give it to him' may become reduced as far as *avng koḍu* (cf. *OCK* p. 14–15, §§2.3, 2.4; Nayak p. 70, rule 1, and pp. 71–72, rule 1). It should be noted that certain short vowels which one would expect to be lost are in fact retained, e.g., the medial *a*'s of *prakaṭa* 'issue' and *duradṛṣṭa* 'bad luck'. The fact that Sanskrit prefixal morphemes are involved in such examples suggests that these examples should be regarded as containing junctures in their underlying forms: *pra+kaṭa, dur+a+dṛṣṭa*. The rule for vowel loss will then apply only to vowels in the environment after VC_n, but not after $+C_n$ (where C_n = one or more consonants).

(14) After vowel loss has taken place, resulting consonant clusters may be simplified, as by degemination: a geminate consonant becomes single when next to a single consonant, e.g., *ibb-aru* 'two people' → *ibbru* → *ibru* (*OCK* p. 15, §2.5; Nayak p. 71, rule 2).

(15) Similarly, a homorganic cluster of nasal plus stop, coming to precede another consonant, loses its stop: *nambida* 'he believed' → *nambda* → *namda* (*OCK*, p. 15, §2.5). This rule creates a contrast, in the surface phonetics, between [ŋ] and the other nasals, as in *hengasu* 'woman' → *hengsu* → *heŋsu;* but the taxonomic phonemic analyses of both my book and Nayak's are misleading in suggesting that *ŋ* is on a par with the other nasal phonemes.

(16) Certain other consonant clusters show assimilation. Laterals assimilate to the position of a preceding retroflex or dental: *kēḷ-ali* 'let him ask' → *kēḷḷi;*[9] *idd-aḷu* 'she was' → *idḷu* → *idlu* (*OCK* pp. 17–18, §2.11.1; Nayak p. 72, rules 6 and 11).

(17) In many dialects, an assimilatory change affects vowels in the first syllables of stems, whereby long and short *e* and *o* have lower allophones [æ] and [ɔ] when a non-high vowel occurs in the next syllable. This development is only sporadically found in Bangalore, but is attested by Nayak's Shimoga data such as *gære* 'line', *nɔre* 'foam' (pp. 44–45). In such cases, the lower vowel quality is, of course, not contrastive. Some dialects also have two qualities of short *a*: [ə] when a high vowel is in the next syllable, [a] elsewhere.

(18) Stem-final *e* becomes *i*—in Bangalore and Shimoga, mainly in verbs; elsewhere, e.g. in Dharwar, in nouns as well. Thus *kare* 'to call' → Ba. *kari,* becoming homonymous with Ba. *kari* 'to fry'. In Shimoga, however, there is a further implication: *bere* 'to mix', which

became *bære* by the previous rule, now becomes *bæri,* and the [æ] becomes contrastive in terms of surface phonetics. Similarly, *ode* 'to kick' → *ɔde* → *ɔdi*. In some dialects the same process also brings [ə] into surface contrast with [a]: Dh. *kari* 'to fry' → *kəri,* vs. *kare* 'to call' → *kari* (cf. Bright 1966a). From the data available, no dialect shows any morphophonemic alternations [e ~ ɛ], [o ~ ɔ], or [ə ~ a] to reflect the historical relationship; on the contrary, they tend to generalize a particular vowel throughout a paradigm. Thus *tar-* 'bring' comes to have [ə] not only before high vowels, as in *tar-ut(t)-ane* 'he brings' → *tərtāne,* but everywhere else as well, e.g. *tənde* 'I brought'—contrasting with *tande* 'father' (*OCK* p. 3, §1.3.5; Nayak p. 45). It appears that, for dialects such as Shimoga and Dharwar, *ɛ ɔ ə* must be recognized as new additions to the systematic-phonemic repertory.

(19) A variety of other phonological rules, of less importance, could be mentioned. E.g., after a lateral, a homorganic *d* is inserted before *r*: *kaḷḷa-ru* 'thieves' → *kaḷru* → *kaḷḍru* (*OCK* p. 18, §2.11.4; Nayak p. 72, rule 13). For other rules, more idiosyncratic to particular dialects, the reader may refer to the sources which have been cited.

(20) The application of rules such as the above will yield broad-phonetic transcriptions for the various colloquial dialects, comparable to the taxonomic-phonemic notations used in my book and Nayak's. Finally, a set of phonetic rules (corresponding to the description in *OCK* pp. 1–5) will account for additional details. Only a few such rules may be noted here: (a) The contrast between short and long vowels is neutralized to half-length when word-final; (b) long vowels in the medial syllables of words are also reduced in length; (c) front vowels /i e/ and back vowels /u o/, whether short or long, tend to have a semivocalic onglide after word boundary, especially when a pause or a vowel precedes (*OCK* p. 15, §2.6).

The above does not pretend to be a full-fledged phonology of any single variety of Kannada, much less of any range of dialects. It is intended rather as a sketch, to suggest what such a fuller description might be like, taking into account that literary and colloquial Kannada are, after all, related to each other in several ways. For one thing, many people have a command of both styles, and even illiterates are able to understand a good deal of literary Kannada, in dramas or sermons; it seems doubtful that speakers draw on completely separate grammars in order to handle the two styles. Furthermore, the literary style represents, to a great extent, a historical source of the colloquial dialects. Finally, its phonology is largely identifiable with the morphophonemic bases of the colloquial dialects; this being the case, it is hardly surprising that even uneducated speakers have a fair passive understanding of the literary language: its phonological structure is already part of their linguistic competence.[10]

NOTES

1. Ferguson uses the terms HIGH and LOW; but I prefer to avoid these because of possible confusion with a different sociolinguistic dimension, that of higher vs. lower social class. The terms LITERARY and COLLOQUIAL are in wide use, but the former term suggests an exclusive association with writing, which is misleading: we might rather refer to FORMAL styles (which are regularly used in speaking, e.g., from the lecture platform) vs. INFORMAL styles (which are increasingly entering literary use).

2. See Dimock (1960), Chatterjee (1962), Shanmugam Pillai (1960, 1965b).

3. See Bright (1958a, hereafter *OCK*); Hiremath (1961), Upadhyaya (1968).

4. Nayak compares literary Kannada with his native colloquial dialect of Shimoga district—although he admits that he has largely replaced the latter by a 'standard colloquial style . . . almost similar to the one described by Bright . . .' (p. 34). It might have been preferable to use the better-known urban colloquial standard as the basis for his comparison. A severely negative review of Nayak's book has been published by Shankar Bhat (1968d).

5. Nayak makes this mysterious statement (ibid.): 'The rules are numbered serially. They do not strictly indicate the order of rules, which is an important criterion in Transformational-Generative grammars.'

6. It is of course possible for the morphophonemic basic forms of a colloquial dialect to be quite distinct from the literary equivalents. E.g., Nayak (p. 38) lists /f s ś z/ as occurring only in his literary style; thus he presumably has basic *dēśa* 'country' in literary style, but basic *dēsa* in colloquial style. In other cases, historical change has reshaped the basic form of the colloquial style; e.g., as shown in section 18 below, Shimoga dialect has basic *ode* 'to kick' in literary style, but basic *ɔdi* in colloquial.

7. He even states (p. 14) that '[linguistic] variation is not necessarily a historical product'.

8. By a later rule, the contrast between short and long vowels is neutralized, in word-final position, to half-length; but morphophonemically long vowels

can be recognized by their immunity to the rules of vowel loss. It may be noted that the literary language allows nominative and genitive case forms in their contracted as well as their full forms, but spelled with final short vowels, as *mane*, etc. (Spencer 1950:55). Nayak's treatment of these data is especially confusing, since he tries to account for the long vowels in noun forms by means of a morpheme *A* (p. 72, rule 14, and p. 77), which he borrows, without explanation, from my 1958 grammar. But if we describe colloquial Kannada in relation to the literary language, the 'real' vowels *a* and *u* can be used instead. Nayak's description of the long vowels in verb forms is even more unfortunate. At one place (p. 72, rule 4), he treats *barītāne* 'he writes' in terms of a rule which seems to say that the second vowel of a stem becomes long before any affix, which is clearly untrue. Elsewhere (pp. 39, 50), he describes the basic long vowel in Shi. *battīni* (Ba. *bartīni*) 'I come' in terms of an ad-hoc juncture (which he ignores in his later discussion of verb morphology).

9. Note that, although our earlier rule (6) eliminated sequences of long vowel before geminate consonant, vowel loss produces such sequences anew, as in the present case.

10. My thanks go to M. B. Emeneau and to M. V. Nadkarni for their constructive criticism of this paper.

7

Hindi Numerals

In most languages encountered by linguists, the numerals, considered as a paradigmatic set, constitute a morpho-syntactic problem of only moderate complexity. Thus, a common pattern, not only in Indo-European but in other families as well, involves single morphemes for numbers 'one' through 'ten', and regular rules of co-occurrence to produce numbers 'eleven' through 'ninety-nine'—with occasional ad hoc morphophonemic statements applying to the teens and the decades, e.g., English *three* → *thir-* in the environment of *-teen* or *-ty*. The description of such numerals can be incorporated with relative ease into a grammar of the larger, open-ended numeral systems of the language concerned.[1]

The Indo-Aryan family of North India presents a curious contrast to such patterns. The relatively regular numeral system of Sanskrit, as it has developed historically into the modern languages of this group, has undergone striking phonological alteration. Morphemes which had relatively uniform shapes and clear boundaries in the parent language have, in this process, become fused and difficult to identify—a reversal of the general Indo-European trend away from more fusional constructions and toward more agglutinative ones. Witness Table 7.1, which gives partial paradigms in Sanskrit (Whitney 1889:177–79) as compared with modern Gujarati (Cardona 1965:84–85).[2] The irregularity visible even in this small sample is in fact, in modern Indo-Aryan generally,[3] maintained as far as '99'. The result is that anyone who

TABLE 7.1

Sanskrit	Gujarati	Sanskrit	Gujarati
40 *catvaariśat*	*calis*	50 *pancaaśat*	*pəcas*
41 *eka-catvaariśat*	*ektalis*	51 *eka-pancaaśat*	*ekavən*
42 *dvaa-catvaariśat*	*betalis*	52 *dvaa-pancaaśat*	*bavən*
43 *trayaś-catvaariśat*	*tetalis*	53 *trayaḥ-pancaaśat*	*trepan*
44 *catuś-catvaariśat*	*cumalis*	54 *catuḥ-pancaaśat*	*cɔpən*
45 *panca-catvaariśat*	*pistalis*	55 *panca-pancaaśat*	*pə̃cavən*

learns to count in one of these languages—whether native speaker or foreign student—must make a greater learning effort than is usually required for the counting process. Once past '99', the going is easier; there is a monomorphemic word for 'hundred' (e.g., Gujerati *sɔ*), and prediction of higher numerals is then possible (e.g., *car sɔ* '400').

Questions which are of some linguistic interst may be asked with regard to these systems. Is memorization the only factor involved in the learning and production of the paradigm up to 'one hundred'? If so, should a grammar, for the sake of psychological realism, simply list these hundred forms (as, in fact, practical grammars do), with no attempt to state general rules governing their phonological shapes? To put the matter in other terms, should we regard all the forms from '11' to '99' as suppletive? Then we would simply say that the string of morphemes ONE-FIVE-DECADE yields *ekavən* 'fifty-one' in Gujarati, just as we might say that English GO-PAST yields *went*. Or, to take an opposite view, are the Indo-Aryan numerals in fact governed by rules, irregular to be sure, but having SOME degree of generality, which are used by the native speaker and may be stated by the linguist?

The present paper will explore these questions with specific reference to Hindi, in the following steps: a complete set of numerals from one to a hundred will be presented; a morphological analysis of this paradigm will be attempted; and finally, the value of the analysis will be discussed. However, there is one difficulty at the start: namely, that many published sources give alternative forms for the Hindi numerals—and, indeed, virtually every source gives a slightly different set. For example, '67' is given variously as *satsaTh* (Harter et al. 1960), *sarsaTh* (Kellogg 1938), and *saRsaTh* (Sharma 1958).[4] The present description is based, to begin with, on the usage of a single informant on a single occasion: Miss Manjari Agrawal, a native Hindi speaker

TABLE 7.2

1 *eek*	21 *ikkiis*	41 *ikyaaliis*	61 *iksaTh*	81 *ikyaasii*
2 *doo*	22 *baaiis*	42 *byaaliis*	62 *baasaTh*	82 *byaasii*
3 *tiin*	23 *teeiis*	43 *tẽẽtaaliis*	63 *treesaTh*	83 *teeraasii*
4 *caar*	24 *caubiis*	44 *cãũtaaliis*	64 *causaTh*	84 *cauraasii*
5 *pããc*	25 *pacciis*	45 *pãĩtaaliis*	65 *pãĩsaTh*	85 *picyaasii*
6 *chee*	26 *chabbiis*	46 *cheeyaaliis*	66 *chyaasaTh*	86 *chyaasii*
7 *saat*	27 *sataaiis*	47 *sãĩtaaliis*	67 *saRsaTh*	87 *sataasii*
8 *aaTh*	28 *aThaaiis*	48 *aRtaaliis*	68 *aRsaTh*	88 *aThaasii*
9 *nau*	29 *untiis*	49 *unancaas*	69 *unahtar*	89 *unaanbee*
10 *das*	30 *tiis*	50 *pacaas*	70 *sattar*	90 *nabbee*
11 *gyaarah*	31 *ikattiis*	51 *ikyaavan*	71 *ikahtar*	91 *ikyaanbee*
12 *baarah*	32 *battiis*	52 *baavan*	72 *bahattar*	92 *byaanbee*
13 *teerah*	33 *tããtiis*	53 *treepan*	73 *teehattar*	93 *teeraanbee*
14 *caudah*	34 *cãũtiis*	54 *cauvan*	74 *cauhattar*	94 *cauraanbee*
15 *pandrah*	35 *pãĩtiis*	55 *pacpan*	75 *pichyattar*	95 *picyaanbee*
16 *soolah*	36 *chattiis*	56 *chappan*	76 *chyattar*	96 *chyaanbee*
17 *satrah*	37 *sãĩtiis*	57 *sataavan*	77 *satattar*	97 *sataanbee*
18 *aThaarah*	38 *aRtiis*	58 *aThaavan*	78 *aThattar*	98 *aThaanbee*
19 *unniis*	39 *untaaliis*	59 *unsaTh*	79 *unaasii*	99 *ninyaanbee*
20 *biis*	40 *caaliis*	60 *saaTh*	80 *assii*	100 *sau*

from Delhi, was asked to count to a hundred at a 'normal' speed, and the results were tape-recorded and transcribed.

Subsequent discussion with Miss Agrawal revealed alternative forms in her usage—though not as much free variation as the published sources suggest. The attested variations will be taken into consideration at a later stage in this discussion; but first, let us consider the tape-recorded forms and their analysis (Table 7.2).[5]

The question of what morphemes are present in these forms, and in what combinations they occur, is the simpler part of our analysis. There are thirteen minimum meaningful elements, falling into several classes. Each of the following morphemes constitutes a distributional class in itself.

TEN, phonologically *das* in isolation.
MINUS ONE, with the usual shape *un-*.
DECADE, with no uniform phonological shape.
HUNDRED, invariably *sau*.

TABLE 7.3

	Unit$_a$	*Unit*$_b$
ONE *eek*	+	–
TWO *doo*	+	+
THREE *tiin*	+	+
FOUR *caar*	+	+
FIVE *pããc*	+	+
SIX *chee*	+	+
SEVEN *saat*	+	+
EIGHT *aaTh*	+	+
NINE *nau*	–	–

The remaining morphemes belong to the general class of UNITS, and are further subject to two intersecting sub-classifications, as in Table 7.3 (phonological shapes given are those occurring in isolation).[6]

The given numeral paradigm may then be generated by the following rules. The numerals produced by each part of the rule are indicated in the right column of Table 7.4.[7]

The above rules do not, however, account for the phonological shapes of our data, where the major complexities lie. We may ask first, then: is it possible to regard these forms as composed of successive phonological strings? In two cases, the answer is clearly positive: MINUS ONE

TABLE 7.4

NUMERAL →	{ UNIT / NUMERAL COMPLEX / HUNDRED }	'1–9' '10–99' '100'
NUMERAL COMPLEX →	{ (UNIT$_a$) + TEN	'10–18'
	({ UNIT$_a$ / MINUS ONE }) + DECADE COMPLEX	'20, 30, . . . 80' '21–28, . . . 81–88' '19, 29, . . . 79'
	({ UNIT / MINUS ONE }) + NINETY }	'90' '91–99' '89'
DECADE COMPLEX →	UNIT$_b$ + DECADE	'20, 30, . . . 80'
NINETY →	NINE + DECADE	'90'

and HUNDRED appear invariably as *un-* and *sau,* respectively. However, to go to the other extreme, the DECADE morpheme, though correlated with a string *-iis* in *biis* '20', *tiis* '30', *caaliis* '40', clearly cannot be assigned any non-arbitrary phonological shape in *pacaas* '50', *saaTh* '60', and the rest. We must, then, consider the combinations of UNIT and DECADE as suppletive in shape, generated by rules such as TWO — DECADE → *biis* and SIX — DECADE → *saaTh.*

Combinations of UNITS with TEN, and with the DECADE COMPLEXES as suppletively produced, must then be accounted for. All of these forms are, in fact, divisible into successive morphemes, if one allows enough allomorphic variation. It is clear that one would prefer those morpheme cuts which yield the lowest allomorph count. Some choices are easy: *saaTh* '60' appears in the allomorph *-saTh* after all UNITS. Other choices are difficult, as in the following forms:

ikyaaliis '41'	*ikyaavan* '51'
byaaliis '42'	*baavan* '52'

Here, apparently, there are common elements *iky-* '1', *-aaliis* '40', *-aavan* '50'; only for the morpheme TWO would we have to recognize allomorphs *by-* and *b-*. But looking further in the data, we find:

cãũtaaliis '44'	*cauvan* '54'

These forms suggest that perhaps the element meaning '50' is *-van* instead of *-aavan,* in which case we must recognize a morph *ikyaa-* 'one' in *ikyaavan* '51'. We can, in fact, recognize the same *ikyaa-* in *ikyaaliis* '41', with a general morphophonemic rule, *aa* + *aa* → *aa,* applying to its combination with *-aaliis* '40' (which is independently identifiable in *cheeyaaliis* '46'). In a few cases, however, only an arbitrary morpheme cut can be made; e.g, in *unancaas* '49', *unan-* would be a unique alternant of *un-* 'minus one', but *-ancaas* is a similarly unique alternant of *pacaas* '50'.

After a good deal of trial-and-error, one can arrive at a description of minimum complexity. The one which follows contains two types of rules: (1) those which state the allomorphs of particular morphemes, and (2) those which state morphophonemic replacements operating throughout the system. Some of the latter rules apply through the entire language; others are more limited.

The allomorphic rules are as shown in Table 7.5.[8]

TABLE 7.5

ONE *eek* →	*gyaa-* / — TEN
	ik- / — '20, 60, 70'
	ikaX- / — '30'
	ikyaa- / — '40, 50, 80, 90'
TWO *doo* →	*baa-* / — {TEN / '20, 50, 60'}
	baX- / — '30, 70'
	by- / — '40, 80, 90' (all cases before *aa*)
THREE *tiin* →	*tee-* / — {TEN / '20, 40, 70'}
	tai- / — '30'
	tree- / — '50, 60'
	teer- / — '80, 90' (all cases before *aa*)
FOUR *caar* →	*cau-* / — {TEN / '20, 30, 40, 50, 60, 70'}
	caur- / — '80, 90' (all cases before *aa*)
FIVE *pããc* →	*pand-* / — TEN
	pac- / — '20, 50'
	pãĩ- / — '30, 40, 60'
	picy- / — '70, 80, 90'
SIX *chee* →	*soo-* / — TEN
	chaX- / — '20, 30, 50'
	chyaa- / — '60'
	chy- / — '70, 80, 90'
SEVEN *saat* →	*sat-* / — {TEN / '70, 80, 90'}
	sataa- / '20, 50'
	sai- / — '30, 40'
	saR- / — '60'
EIGHT *aaTh* →	*aThaa-* / — {TEN / '20, 50'}
	aR- / — '30, 40, 60'
	aTh- / — '70, 80, 90'
NINE *nau* →	*niny-* / — '90'
TEN *das* →	*-rah* / '1, 2, 3, 5, 7, 8' —
	-dah / '4' —
	-lah / '6' —
biis 'twenty' →	*-Xiis* / — {MINUS ONE / '1, 2, 3, 5, 7, 8'} —

Mtiis 'thirty' has no allomorphic alternation.

TABLE 7.5 Cont.

caaliis 'forty' →	*-Mtaaliis* / $\left\{\begin{array}{l}\text{MINUS ONE}\\ \text{'3, 4, 5, 7, 8'}\end{array}\right\}$ —
	-aaliis / '1, 2, 6' —
pacaas 'fifty' →	*-ancaas* / MINUS ONE —
	-van / '1, 2, 4, 7, 8' —
	-pan / '3, 5, 6' —
saaTh 'sixty' →	*-saTh* / $\left\{\begin{array}{l}\text{MINUS ONE}\\ \text{UNIT}\end{array}\right\}$ —
sattar 'seventy' →	*-ahtar* / $\left\{\begin{array}{l}\text{MINUS ONE}\\ \text{'1'}\end{array}\right\}$ —
	-hattar / '2, 3, 4, 5, 6, 7, 8' —
assii 'eighty' →	*-aasii* / $\left\{\begin{array}{l}\text{MINUS ONE}\\ \text{UNIT}\end{array}\right\}$ —
nabbee 'ninety' →	*-aanbee* / $\left\{\begin{array}{l}\text{MINUS ONE}\\ \text{UNIT}\end{array}\right\}$ —

The morphophonemic rules, with examples, are the following.

(1) *X* + *C* → *CC* (otherwise *X* → Ø)
ik- '1' + *-Xiis* '20' → *ikkiis* '21'
chaX- '6' + *biis* '20' → *chabbiis* '26'
(2) *VV* + *M* → *ṼṼ* (otherwise *M* → Ø)
cau- '4' + *-Mtiis* '30' → *cãũtiis* '34'
(3) *aa* + *aa* → *aa*[9]
ikyaa- '1' + *-aasii* '80' → *ikyaasii* '81'
(4) *ee* + *aa* → *eeyaa*[10]
chee '6' + *-aaliis* '40' → *cheeyaaliis* '46'
(5) *Cy* + *h* → *Chy*
picy- '5' + *-hattar* '70' → *pichyattar* '75'
(6) *Ch* + *h* → *Ch*
aTh- '8' + *-hattar* '70' → *aThattar* '78'

If a somewhat different set of forms had been used, e.g., those presented in any particular textbook of Hindi, the details of this description would of course be different; but the general outlines, and the approximate degree of complexity, would be the same. Having arrived at this point, we are still faced with these questions: is such an analysis meaningful, or worth doing? Does it correspond to any reality in the competence of the Hindi speaker who uses these forms?

We may refer, in this connection, to the discussion of related issues by Garvin (1961) and by Voegelin (1962). The former author, presenting a complex problem in the morphological analysis of Palauan, raises this question: how does the linguist, on the practice level, make a non-arbitrary choice between alternative analyses, each of which achieves some sort of economy? His answer is: one chooses that solution which 'yields results of the kind that allow the analyst to suspect the presence of general conditions in the language rather than merely particular conditions pertaining to the sample at hand' (Garvin 1961:68). Commenting on Garvin's article, Voegelin (1962:47) makes the point that the dictionary of a language, rather than the grammar, is the proper 'repository for irregularities' such as our rules of Hindi allomorphy. But these authors are focussing on the question of alternative segmentations of morphological data, and of resulting degrees of generality and economy in linguistic statement; they are not explicitly raising the issue of psychological validity which I wish to consider here. From my point of view, the question is this: is it meaningful to make ANY segmentation of the Hindi numerals into specified phonological strings? Or is it more realistic to simply list the entire set of forms, with the implication that native speakers produce them entirely from memory, rather than by application of rules? If the answer is to be obtained purely on the basis of economy in description, then we might reason as follows: in the description given above, there are 184 items which represent phonological shapes or specific environments. If, on the other hand, we give a simple list of the phonological shapes of forms—in effect, an ad hoc rule for each form—then, of course, there would be just 100 items, with a clear advantage in economy. But we have no guarantee that economy in rules is a simple or unique reflection of psychological reality.

I would like to suggest that the great variability in the phonological shapes of the Hindi numerals—a characteristic as striking as their morphological complexity—may bear on the question which has been posed. Some degree of free variation, of the type of English /ìykənámiks ~ èkənámiks/, may, of course, be expected to characterize languages in general. Hindi, as a language which has numerous geographical and social dialects, and which is not afflicted with a very long-established or rigidified literary standard, will show a certain amount of such free variation, even in the most homogeneous style. It is surprising, however, to find such an extreme range of variation in the numeral system, going much beyond that found in other types of words. It is clear that if these numeral forms were learned simply by memorization, and produced out of memory without any other conflicting factors, then the multiplicity of alternate forms could never come into existence. This appears to indicate that factors other than memory ARE to be considered in the description of the Hindi numerals.

One factor seems to be the influence of adjacent forms in the sequence of counting (cf. footnote 4 of this article). Consider again the allomorphs of SEVEN *saat* in the numeral '67', variously pronounced as *satsaTh, sarsaTh,* and *saRsaTh.* Of these pronunciations, the first seems to be historically the most conservative, with preservation of *t*. The second shows a weakening of *t* to *r*, a process which has parallels elsewhere. The third, however, shows a retroflex articulation, which has no historical justification if we consider this word as an isolate. Looking at it in the counting sequence, however, we observe that *saRsaTh* '67' may well have arisen on the model of *aRsaTh* '68', where the retroflex is historically 'right'. Can we say, then, that the speaker who uses *saRsaTh* is doing so in conformity to a RULE, perhaps one of 'distant assimilation of retroflexes'? Such a statement does not seem profitable, since in fact this rule would have as little generality as the alternative ad hoc statements that *saat* → *saR-* before '60', or simply that '7' + '60' → *saRsaTh.*

There are, however, examples of other kinds. The numeral '63' is given as *treesaTh* or *tirsaTh* by most published sources, but as *teesaTh* by Harter et al. (1960). A simple assimilation to neighboring *baasaTh* '62' or following *causaTh* '64' cannot be postulated in this case. Instead, we may suppose that Harter's informant was using a rule which has already been recognized, namely THREE *tiin* → *tee-*, but that he applied it in an expanded set of environments—not only before TEN and before '20', '40', '70', but before '60' as well. The production of such forms as *teesaTh* '63' may thus be understood not in terms of a new rule, but rather in terms of the rules given above, with some reshuffling in the statement of environments.

As college students of elementary Hindi can readily attest, these numerals are hard to learn, and they cannot be that much easier for the native speaker. In either case, much must be memorized. Some things are easy to remember, e.g., that *saaTh* '60' becomes *-saTh* after all elements; because this is so easy, not a single source shows any variation in the shape of this *-saTh*. But it is hard to remember that THREE *tiin* becomes *tee-* in certain environments, *tai-* in others, *tir-* in still others. When memory becomes confused, a rule like *tiin* → *tee-* may be applied in a novel environment. But such changes cannot be explained unless we accept that allomorphic rules DO exist for the production of these forms.

My conclusion is this: where linguistic data are extremely complex, the simplest description, measured by economy of symbols, may be a simple list. But such a list is not the only possible psychological reality. Where partial similarities of meaning and phonological shape exist between forms, they can be perceived by the native speaker as well as by the linguist. These patterns, messy as they may be, can be formulated as implicit rules in the head of the speaker, just as they can be formulated as explicit rules by the linguist. The amount of variation which can be observed in the Hindi numerals is in part a manifestation of those implicit rules, and of their unusual complexity.

NOTES

1. Such grammars have recently been published for Dutch by Katwijk (1965), for English by Brainerd (1966), and for Chinese by Kelkar (1966). See also Brandt Corstius (1968).

2. Transcriptions are normalized for comparability with that used here for Hindi.

3. A glance at some grammars of modern Indo-Aryan languages indicates that such systems occur at least in Bengali, Marathi, and Punjabi, as well as Hindi and Gujarati. They do not occur in the Dravidian languages, nor in Singhalese—which, though Indo-Aryan, is spoken far to the south, in Ceylon.

4. The notation used here for Hindi words is that of Harter et al. (1960).

5. In general, these forms fall within the range of variation which is attested in textbooks of Hindi. A few, however, may be novel. For '41', *ikyaaliis,* instead of the commonly reported *iktaaliis,* may have arisen by analogy with following *byaaliis* '42' (one is reminded of the well-known contamination of numerals in other languages, e.g. PIE **kwetwó:res, *pénk^{w}e* > Latin *quattuor, quinque,* English *four, five*—to cite Bloomfield [1933:422–423]). For '44', *cãũtaaliis,* instead of unnasalized *cautaaliis,* seems to reflect influence of neighboring *tẽẽtaaliis* '43' and *pãĩtaaliis* '45'. For '49', *unancaas* stands alongside more standard *uncaas;* cf. Punjabi *uninjaa* (Hares 1929). The forms *unahtar* '69' and *ikahtar* '71' diverge from standard *unhattar* and *ikhattar* through a modified application of the rule which drops medial *a*'s in the prototypes **unahattar* and **ikahattar.* For '75', *pichyattar,* by comparison with standard *pachattar,* shows inserted *y* on the model of following *chyattar* '76', as well as the effect on the first vowel of the palatals which adjoin it. For '85' and '95', *picyaasii* and *picyaanbee,* alongside more standard *pacaasii* and *pacaanbee,* again show *y* on the model of *chyaasii* '86' and *chyaanbee* '96'. For '89', *unaanbee* shows the element *un-* 'minus one', which is normal in '19, 29, 39, ... 79'—though the textbooks give *navaasii*; Punjabi influence is again possible. The numbers '91' through '99' show an element *-nbee* '90', where most sources give *-nvee.*

6. The minus signs indicate that, although an element belongs to the general class of UNITS, it does not belong to the particular subclass.

7. The plus is used here as a concatenation symbol.

8. It is understood that the element on the left-hand side of the rule will remain unchanged if no environment on the right-hand side is applicable; thus *eek* in isolation remains *ee*. The morphophonemic symbol *X* is here introduced, with the meaning 'doubling of adjacent single consonant' (specified by morphophonemic rule 1, below), e.g. in *ikaX* '30'. In reference to NINE *nau* → *niny-*, note that this morpheme does not occur in any other decade complex. The morphophonemic symbol *M* means 'nasalization of preceding vowel' (by rule 2 below), e.g. in *Mtiis* 'thirty'.

9. This rule is valid for Sanskrit, and thus for many learned compounds borrowed into Hindi, e.g., *dayaanand* 'bliss of grace' (used as a personal name) *dayaa* 'grace' + *aanand* 'bliss'. In Hindi verbal morphology, however, a *y* is inserted in such sequences, e.g., *aayaa* 'he came' < *aa-* 'come' + *-aa* '3rd sing. masc. preterit'.

10. The *y* is non-contrastive in this position, in the language as a whole, and could in fact be omitted from phonemic notation.

8

The Dravidian Enunciative Vowel

Introduction

1. Phonological accounts of modern Indian languages are currently entering what may be thought of as their third period. In this reckoning, the first period would be the 'Pre-Structuralist', in which the indigenous orthographies were taken as the basis for description; well-known Dravidian examples are the 'pronunciation' sections of Arden (1934) for Tamil, or of Spencer (1950) for Kannada. The second period, characterized by 'Structuralist' descriptions, focused on pronunciation rather than orthography, and attempted to classify phonetic segments into PHONEMES, frequently observing such Neo-Bloomfieldian commandments as 'Once a phoneme, always a phoneme' and 'Thou shalt not mix levels.' Typical examples are the phonemic descriptions of Fowler (1954) for Tamil and Bright (1958a) for Kannada. The third period, which we now find upon us, can be called the 'Generative' period, and the new emphasis is on partially ordered phono-

This chapter is a revised version of my article 'The enunciative vowel', which was published in the *International Journal of Dravidian Linguistics* (Bright 1972a). The present version incorporates material from the discussion published in Bright 1973.

logical rules that lead from underlying phonological strings to the surface phonetics. It is widely felt that this generative phonology has many advantages over its predecessor: it accounts for both morphophonemics and allophonics without imposing artificial divisions; it aims at correspondence with psychological reality, and sometimes succeeds; it achieves degrees of economy and generalization that were inaccessible to the older approach; it shows certain interesting relationships with findings of historical linguistics; and it provides a lucid format for description of dialect variation, geographical or social. Examples, again for Tamil and Kannada, respectively, are Bright and Lindenfeld (1968), Bright (1970).

Two examples from my own work may be given. Kannada has a segment [ŋ] that occurs in all styles before velar stops: [beŋki] 'fire', [tʌŋgi] 'younger sister'. In literary Kannada (LK), it is in complementary distribution with [n]; thus phonemic transcriptions *benki, tangi* are justifiable for that style. But as we move from literary to colloquial Kannada (CK), the situation changes. In many cases, LK short vowel corresponds to CK zero, as in LK [mʌgəḷu], CK [mʌgḷu] 'daughter'; and CK often shows simplification of resulting consonant clusters, as in LK [hɛŋgəsu], CK [hɛŋsu] 'wife'. In CK, then, [ŋ] is no longer predictable in terms of the following surface segment; in my earlier work, agreeing with Biligiri (1955), I therefore set up a CK phoneme /ŋ/, and wrote phonemically not only /heŋsu/, but also /beŋki/ and /taŋgi/. Now, however, I would prefer to account for both LK and CK facts in the following set of rules: (1) In all styles, basic *n* becomes [ŋ] before velars. (2) In CK, medial short vowels are lost. (3) In the cluster nasal + stop + obstruent, the stop is lost. In this description, 'wife' is basically *hengas*. Final *u* is added by the 'enunciative vowel' rule—which will be the main topic of this paper. By our present rule 1, *hengasu* is realized as *heŋgasu*—which, with the operation of low-level phonetic rules, is the CK pronunciation. By rule 2, CK then has *heŋgsu*—and one does sometimes hear the *g;* but normally, rule 3 operates to produce *heŋsu* (compare Bright 1970, rule 15).

A second example is from Sanskrit. At the height of the 'Structuralist' period, I described visarga, the voiceless [ḥ], as an allophone of voiced *h,* on the basis of complementary distribution in surface phonetics (Bright 1958b). But this analysis obscures both the morphophonemic and the historical relationship of visarga with *s*. I would still say that visarga is not a 'phoneme'—that is, not one of the basic phonological units of Sanskrit; but I would derive it from basic *s* as is done by traditional sandhi rules, rather than from voiced *h*.

The Enunciative Vowel

2. The model of generative phonology will, when fully applied, suggest many other modifications in the phonemic analyses of Indian languages. Here I wish to give attention to a particular set of analytical problems that arises in the Dravidian languages. As the pronunciation of these languages does not display obstruents before pause, loan words from Indo-Aryan or English regularly take an added vowel, for example, *pariṣattu* 'society', *bassu* 'bus'. This vowel is usually pronounced as [ï] in Tamil, Malayalam, Tulu, and in some Kannada dialects of North Karnatak;[1] it is usually pronounced as [u] in other dialects of Kannada and in Telugu. In the orthographies of most of the literary languages, it is written as *u*. This is called by Caldwell the 'enunciative vowel', and his discussion ([1913] 1956:134–35) is worth quoting in its entirety:

> In the Dravidian languages, . . . short *u* is of all vowels the weakest and lightest, and is largely used, especially at the end of words, for euphonic purposes, or as a help to enunciation. In grammatical written Telugu, every word without exception must end in a vowel; and if it has not naturally a vowel ending of its own, *u* is to be suffixed to the last consonant. This rule applies even to Sanskrit derivatives; and the neuter abstracts ending in *-m,* which have been borrowed from Sanskrit, must end in *m-u* in Telugu. Though this *u* is always written, it is often dropped in pronunciation. In modern Canarese a similar rule holds. . . . The Tamil rule, with regard to the addition of *u* to words which end in a consonant, accords with the rule of the ancient Canarese. The rule is, that in words which end in any hard or surd consonant, viz., in *k, ch, ṭ, t,* or *p* (each of which is the leading consonant of a varga), or in the hard, rough *ṟ,* which is peculiar to these languages, the hard consonant shall be followed by *u* (as *q* by *sh'vā* in Hebrew), in consequence of its being impossible for Tamilian organs of speech to pronounce those letters without the help of a succeeding vowel. In most instances this enunciative *u* is not merely short, but so very short that its quality is determined by grammarians to be equal only to a fourth of the quality of a long vowel. . . . In modern colloquial Tamil, *u* is suffixed to al-

> most every final consonant—to the semi-vowels and nasals, as well as the surds; and even in the ancient or classical Tamil it is sometimes suffixed to final *l*—for example, *śol(l)-u*, speak, instead of simply *śol*. The employment of *u* in the manner and for the purposes now mentioned is obviously quite foreign to Indo-European usages. It is not derived from Sanskrit, and is opposed to Sanskrit laws of sound. It will be termed the ENUNCIATIVE *u* . . .

More recent discussions of the Dravidian enunciative vowel have been published by Ramaswami Aiyar (1935), by K. Kanapathi Pillai (1943), and by M. B. Emeneau (1970:153). These accounts are consistent with the general picture presented by Caldwell; further reference will be made to them below with respect to particular languages.

The above facts suggest, then, that the enunciative vowel is wholly predictable by rule, and that it corresponds to zero in the underlying phonological structure. Then we would have stems with basic shapes such as Kannada *kās* 'coin', becoming *kāsu* by a rule of this approximate form:

$$\emptyset \rightarrow u \;/\; \text{obstruent} \;\_\_\_\; \#$$

Phonemic descriptions that ascribe to the final *u* in *bassu* 'bus' the same status as the stem-*u* would, in this view, be called into question.

3. Several problems surround this vowel, however. Let us consider some of them:

3.1. In Tamil (as mentioned by Caldwell) and in Malayalam, some words lack the enunciative vowel in the literary style, but have it in the colloquial; for example, lit. *kāl*, colloq. *kālï* 'quarter'.[2] The colloquial dialects have a more general rule for the enunciative vowel. In them, it occurs not only after obstruents, but after any consonant.[3]

3.2. In Tamil, Malayalam, and Kannada, some words have final *-y* in the literary style, but *-yi* in the colloquial; for example, lit. *nāy* 'dog', colloq. *nāyi*. Here, evidently, the rule operates which adds an enunciative vowel after any consonant; but after the high front semivowel *y*, the vowel added is fronted to *i* (compare Bright 1970, rule 8).

3.3. In many dialects (e.g. in Tamil, Malayalam, and Tulu), where the utterance-final enunciative vowel is usually unrounded [ï], a similar nonfront unrounded vowel is also found in utterance-medial position, in many dialects: e.g., colloq. Tamil *kaṭṭïkrẽ* 'I tie'. We may ask: if the final [ï] has no contrastive status, what about the medial [ï]?

3.4. In several languages, some occurrences of final *u* or *ï* show stable morphophonemic behavior, unlike that of the enunciative; e.g. Ka. *magu* 'child', accusative *maguvanna*—cf. *kāḍu* 'forest', accusative *kāḍanna*. Such words are best regarded as having basic final *u;* before a vowel, the glide *v* is interpolated by a very general process (Bright 1970, rule 10). In some Tamil-Malayalam dialects, by a later rule, *u* then becomes [ï] before word boundary; see §4.2 below.

3.5. In various dialects, especially in Malayalam and Tulu, there is surface contrast between [u] and [ï] before word boundary. Recent phonemic descriptions of these languages (S. Upadhyaya 1969, Shankar Bhat 1967) set up separate phonemes /u/ and /ï/, but these are found only in limited types of environment. The question arises as to whether this distinction can be made redundant by use of a generative description. The matter is discussed in §§7–9 below.

3.7. In some styles of these languages, [ï] occurs in a sequence [rï], but other styles have [ru]; e.g. [rïtu], [rutu] 'season'. All examples are Sanskrit loanwords, in which Sanskrit originally had a syllabic *r̥*. Their basic forms may be regarded as still having such a unit, realized as [rï] or [ru] by rules of the modern languages (cf. Bright 1970, rule 3).

3.8. In various dialects of Tamil, and typically in Koḍagu, front vowels in word-initial syllables are retracted to central position when followed by retroflex consonants; thus Ta. *vīḍï* 'house' becomes [vï·ḍï], where the first [ï] is central, the second is back. But in Koḍagu, at least, the short [ï] so resulting may be phonetically the same as enunciative [ï], creating an analytic problem of 'overlapping phonemes'.

3.9. In the following sections, the details of these problems will be presented for a number of Dravidian languages, with reference to available dialect data. The aim will be to uphold the generalization that the enunciative vowel, in spite of various historical changes, remains a nonbasic, predictable feature of Dravidian phonology, and that contrasts of [ï] and [u] are a matter of surface structure, not deep structure. For many languages and dialects, sufficient data are not at hand to clarify all the problems mentioned in §§3.1–3.7; however, the general outlines are clear in most cases, and will be summarized in §14.

Tamil

4.1. The earliest description of the Tamil enunciative vowel is that given in Tolkāppiyam, where E̱luttatikāram, sūtras 1–2 (following the edition and translation of Subrahmanya Sastri 1930) speak of 'secondary' *u* (that is *ï*); this is said (sūtra 36) to appear 'as the final member after a hard consonant [i.e., an obstruent] in words having a long vowel before it (like *nākï* [''cow'']) or in *toṭarmoḻi* (like *teṅkï* [''coconut tree''], *varakï* [''grain sp.''], etc.)'. The technical term toṭarmoḻi is explained (sūtra 45) as a 'word having more than two letters'—i.e. akṣaras or (C)V sequences in the written system, as in *te-ṅ-kï, va-ra-kï*. This is expanded in sūtra 407:

> There are only six kinds of words where *ï* is found. They are īreḻuttorumoḻi or words like *nāki* or *īṟï* ['end'] made up of two vowel-consonants;[4] uyirttoṭarmoḻi or words like *varakï* or *aracï* ['king'] having a vowel-consonant between the first vowel or vowel-consonant and the last vowel-consonant; iṭaittoṭarmoḻi or words like *teḷkï* ['flea'] or *eḷḷï* ['sesamum'] having a semivowel [i.e., a sonorant or resonant] between the first vowel-consonant or vowel in the last vowel-consonant; āytattoṭarmoḻi or words like *ehkï* ['steel'] or *kahcï* ['a weight'] having an āytam [h] between the first vowel or vowel-consonant and the last vowel-consonant; vanroṭarmoḻi or words like *kokkï* ['crane'] or *eṭṭï* ['eight'] having a voiceless consonant between the first vowel-consonant or vowel and the last vowel-consonant; and menroṭarmoḻi or words like *teṅkï* or *eṅkï* ['where'] having a nasal between the first vowel-consonant or vowel and the last vowel-consonant.'

That is, Tolkāppiyam describes [ï] as occurring after final obstruents in all words EXCEPT those of shape (C)VCV, e.g. *puḻu* 'worm'; by implication, such words must have rounded *u*.

4.2. The Tamil enunciative vowel, both as described by grammatical tradition and as used in modern speech, was discussed by Ramaswami Aiyar (1935:91–94) as follows:

> Final *ï* of Tamil, described as kuṟṟiyal-ukaram (shortened *u*) and possessing the sound-value of an unrounded *u* . . . is elided altogether in Tamil when it meets the initial vowel of a following word within pause limits in prose and verse-units in poetry.

> The occurrence of this *ï* is described in TE [Tolkāppiyam-Eḻutatikāram], 36, 407 and N [Naṉṉūl], 94. It appears finally after the plosives (or the affricates) of forms having more than two syllables and of dissyllabic forms when these have long base-vowels: *āṟï* (river), . . . *kayirï* (rope), . . . *kokkï* (stork), . . . *ampï* (arrow), . . . *koytï* (having reaped) . . . The sound occurs, according to grammatical tradition, only after the plosives (including *ṟ* and *c* which are always classified as plosives), so much so that in forms like *aḷavu* (measurement) or *puṟavu* (dove) the sound cannot be *ï* but only *u*. In all dissyllabic words with a short basic vowel, whether immediately followed by short plosives or other short consonants, the final vowel is *u* or muṟṟiyal-ukaram, as in *puḻu* (worm), *naṭu* (middle) . . .
>
> The indigenous grammarians are quite definite about the distinction between the contexts where *u* should occur and those where *ï* is prescribed. The distinction is important in the literary dialect in sandhi. But in the colloquial, the sound *ï* has become more widespread, and in actual evaluation the colloquial uses *ï* for all u-karam sounds except in a few dissyllabic words like *puḻu* (worm), *kocu* (mosquito) in which the muṟṟiyal-ukaram or full *u* is preserved as the final on account of the influence of the rounded vowels preceding . . . *naṭu* (middle), *viṭu* (leave off!), etc. are evaluated in the colloquial as . . . *naḍï, viḍï,* etc. . . .
>
> In literary sandhi, *ï* is elided before another following vowel, while muṟṟiyal-ukaram *u* does not suffer this elision.
>
> The general rule of the non-elision of muṟṟiyal-ukaram (= fully rounded *u*) is subject to . . . exceptions . . . Forms like *puṟavu* (dove), *naṟavu* (toddy), *aḷavu* (measurement), according to the rule regarding final *u* and *ï*, have a fully rounded *-u*; but before vowels following, this *u* is invariably elided even in the most ancient texts . . .
>
> It will be seen later that in vocalic sandhi action the kuṟṟiyal-ukaram *ï* of Tamil corresponds to the elidable *ï* of Malayalam, to the elidable *-u* of Kannada, and to *-ï* (or *-u* in some contexts) of Tulu, while the muṟṟiyal-ukaram *u* of Tamil, generally speaking, answers to a non-elidable *-u* of Mal., Kann. and Tulu. Literary Tamil, Mal., and to a certain extent Tulu also distinguish the two in sound-evaluation, while Kann. gives the value of a rounded *u* to both the elidable and the non-elidable sounds. . . .

If we try to restate this description in our own terms, we may say that in classical Tamil the enunciative vowel appeared before a non-vowel (i.e. consonant or pause) when preceded by an obstruent. But the modern tendency to use the enunciative vowel even after nonobstruents was apparently already operative in classical Tamil after *v*, thus *aḷav* → *aḷavu* 'measurement'. The phonetic quality of the enunciative was anciently [ï] everywhere except after *v*, where it was *u*. On the other hand, underlying stem-final *u* has always occurred in examples like *naṭu* 'middle'.[5] In the classical language, this was phonetically rounded; but in some modern colloquial dialects, a late rule normally changes this to [ï], merging phonetically with the enunciative vowel—thus *naḍï*. An exception is found when the preceding vowel is rounded; thus *kocu* 'mosquito' keeps its final rounding.

It should be noted that cases of basic CVC*u* include not only nouns, but verbs like *vaṟu* 'parch', which preserves *u* in past tense *vaṟuttēṉ* 'I parched'.[6] But other verbs like *viṭu* 'leave', pronounced with final [u] by the classical rule, lack the corresponding vowel in many inflected forms (for example *viṭ-ṭēṉ* 'I left'), so that the basic stem seems to be *viṭ*.

4.3. In his paper on 'The enunciative vowel in Dravidian', discussing mainly Tamil, K. Kanapathi Pillai (1943) covers many of the same facts. Referring to the alternation of final [ï] with zero, he writes (pp. 36–37):

> When a word beginning with a vowel follows them, these words [like *nākï* 'cow'] behave as if they ended in consonants. In fact it is possible that words of this kind might have originally ended in consonants, and the *ï* may be a later addition. It is owing to this fact that, when a word with initial vowel comes after it, the Tamil speaker is unconsciously reminded that the preceding word had the consonantal ending, and he simply joins to it the initial vowel of the succeeding word. In this circumstance he entirely forgets the *ï* sound.

Psychologizing aside, it may be seen that K. Kanapathi Pillai's account represents an advance over that of Ramaswami Aiyar. Rather than setting up a final *ï* that is predictable, but must then be elided before vowels, K. Kanapathi Pillai posits that, historically and descriptively, Tamil has words that basically end in an obstruent, for example *nāk*. Before a consonant or pause, the enunciative vowel is inserted by rule; before a vowel, no such process operates.

K. Kanapathi Pillai also notes the use of the enunciative vowel after sonorants (p. 39): 'There are in the Sangam texts a few instances of words ending in this vowel wherein it is joined to consonants other than plosives . . . : *paṇṇï* 'melody', *pullï* 'encircling'. Examples like these are not many in the Sangam texts. But in the later language they are frequently met with . . . : *poṉṉï* 'gold', *villï* 'bow' . . .' The rule inserting the enunciative vowel in this environment is the same as that given above.[7]

Finally, it may be observed that neither Ramaswami Aiyar nor K. Kanapathi Pillai (nor any other of the writers surveyed) provides any detailed information on the occurrence or the pronunciation of the enunciative vowel in word-medial position (this is true not only for Tamil, but for all the Dravidian languages). We may observe that combinations of stems with consonantal suffixes generally show the same vowel that appears before pause: for example, colloq. *villï* 'bow', *villï-haḷ* 'bows'—or, in verbs, *kaṭṭï* 'tie', *kaṭṭï-kr-ẽ* 'I tie'. It is tempting to suggest that medial *ï* is predictable in such cases; but consonant clusters do exist with no interpolated *ï*, for example in *vēṭkai* 'desire', *teḻkï* 'flea' (compare Marr and Kothandaraman 1973). As far as I know, no one has assembled data for any Dravidian dialect that would show the exact relative distribution of word-medial [u], [ï], and zero. In the sections that follow, I report available information on medial vowels, but am obliged to defer conclusions.

5. Descriptive accounts for various modern forms of Tamil tend to report situations like those described above, with occasional minor variations. The relevant literature is surveyed in the following sections.

5.1. One of the first structurally oriented publications on Tamil phonology is that of Firth (1934). Dealing with a literary style of pronunciation, he describes rounded *u* as occurring only in the first syllable of a word; elsewhere, two unrounded vowel phones are said to occur (pp. xxx–xxxi). One of these, close [ï], appears in final position; e.g. *orï* 'one', *neettrï* 'yesterday'. The other, 'half-close' variant occurs before final *m*, e.g. *mattrïm* 'and the other', and in medial syllables, e.g. *koṇḍirïndān* 'he was getting'. It is worth noting that this form of Tamil has final *ï* even in *orï* 'one', where the grammatical tradition calls for rounded *u*.

5.2. In the literary variety described by Fowler (1954:361), *ï* occurs before word juncture, *u* elsewhere; no further details are given.

5.3. The Jaffna dialect of Ceylon Tamil as described by Kuno (1958) (said to be colloquial, but probably in fact a rather formal style), is described as having enunciative [ï] both medially and finally (p. 46).

The vowels *i ī* are said to be have retracted allophones before retroflexes, but not pronounced as far back as the enunciative [ï] (p. 43).

5.4. In what is perhaps the first available structural description of a colloquial Tamil dialect, Subramoniam (1958) reports the dialect of the Vellala community in Nagercoil as having enunciative [ï] in most final positions, but [u] after stems of the shape (C)VC-; thus [u:ḍï] 'transparent' but [uḍu] 'wear' (pp. 12–13). Final [u] and medial [ï] are also noted in certain morphological constructions, e.g. [varïu] 'it comes'.

In his brief Morphophonology section (p. 39), it is clear that Subramoniam is treating the enunciative vowel as derived rather than basic, since he has a rule that 'All C-ending stems except those in *-y* add *-u* [i.e., usually *ï*] before word juncture'; thus *āṭ-* > *āḍï* 'to dance'. (The exclusion of *y* presumably means that stems like *nāy* 'dog' remain without an enunciative vowel; but I can find no explicit statement.) Stems ending in basic *u* are set up, however; all examples noted are of the shape (C)VCV, e.g. *paṭu* 'receive', *karu* 'black'. By the allophonic statement quoted above, these would be pronounced with final [ï].

Cases of alternation between word-final *ï* and word-medial zero are handled by Subramoniam mainly in terms of specific statements of allomorphy; thus the neuter suffix is *-tï* in *adï* 'it', but *-t* in accusative *ade*. It would appear that such phenomena could be better handled in terms of the enunciative vowel.

5.5. In a pioneering series of articles on Tamil dialectology, Kamil Zvelebil has given data on the enunciative vowel for a variety of colloquial dialects.

In one of his earlier reports, for the Madurai dialect, the enunciative vowel is described (Zvelebil 1960a:421–22) as [u] when medial and when final in disyllabic words (e.g. *oru* 'one', *reṇḍu* 'two'); as extra short [ŭ] 'medially usual in polysyllabic words in labial, cacuminal and retroflex environment' and 'finally in polysyllabic items and in free variation in disyllabic words'; and as high back [ï] in remaining environments, including 'medially rarely also in cacuminal or retroflex environments' and 'finally in more than disyllabic words and in disyllabic words after first syllable long'. Short and long *i* in initial syllables are noted as having centralized variants before retroflexes.

In the dialect of Dindigul, the enunciative vowel is reported as [ï] 'medially and finally; finally almost regular . . . in polysyllabic words

. . . however, in disyllabic words also, if first syllable long' (Zvelebil 1961:428). The alternant [ŭ] is listed, presumably as medial, and occurring finally in words of shape (C)VCV. Backed variants of *i ī* are reported 'before cacuminals and retroflexes' (p. 425).

The dialect of Erode is described (Zvelebil 1963c:637–38) as having enunciative [u] medially, and also finally in disyllables, extra short [ŭ] medially and finally, but also [ï] 'frequent medially and finally'. The vowels *i ī* are said to have centralized variants before retroflexes (p. 636).

The dialect of Tuticorin is described (Zvelebil 1963c:650) as having enunciative [u] or [ŭ] medially and finally, but also [ï] with the same distribution. The vowel *i* is said to have a backed variant in all except absolute initial position (p. 649).

The dialect of Ramnad (Zvelebil 1963c:659), has enunciative [u] 'medially, finally in short disyllabic words', or [ŭ] 'in unstressed position medially and finally'; but [ï] is 'the most frequent variant in unstressed position, especially finally'. The vowel *i* is described as backed 'in unstressed syllables, and before cacuminals' (p. 658); in some instances it seems to have merged phonetically with back [ï], as in *piḷḷai* > *pïḷḷe* 'child' (p. 665).

For 'Standard Colloquial Tamil', a type of informal speech said to be used between educated persons throughout Tamil Nad, the enunciative vowel is described as high back [ï] in final position, with a somewhat more central and lower variant in medial position (Zvelebil 1963b:228); no occurrence of final or medial [u] is mentioned. The vowels *i ī* are said to have retracted allophones before retroflexes, but these are phonetically distinguished from the enunciative (p. 227).

5.6. The Srīvaiśnava Brahmin dialect of Madras, as described by Bright and Ramanujan (1962:15–18), has an enunciative *ï*, occurring finally (e.g. *adï* 'it', *rūmï* 'room'), and in a very short variety when medial (e.g. *gōdïme* 'wheat', *varïvā̆* 'he'll come'). But rounded [u] occurs finally and medially in a few examples, e.g. *kosu* 'mosquito', *rāmu* 'nickname for Rāman', *rāmukkï* 'to Rāmu'. In these examples, we must say that *u* is NOT the enunciative vowel, but the basic vowel *u,* rare but not impossible in non-initial syllables.

5.7. In the Tirunelveli dialect, according to Kamatchinathan (1969:9), the enunciative *ï* occurs in most positions; but rounded [u] occurs 'finally in the disyllabic word if preceded by [(C)uC]'—e.g. *kuḍu* 'give'. The sandhi rules (pp. 33–34) refer to the alternation of zero with enunciative *ï* (*kāḍï* 'forest', *kāḍā* 'forest?') and enunciative *u* (*toḍu* 'touch', inf. *toḍa*); but note the stability of the stem-final vowel in words like *pasu* 'cow', *pasuvā* 'cow?' (presumably pronounced with [ï]).

5.8. In Irula, a tribal dialect of the Nilgiris (as reported by Diffloth 1969), front vowels have been retracted before retroflexes, as in dialects mentioned above (§§5.3, 5.5); but subsequent to that change, the retroflex glide *ḻ* is deleted. The result is forms like [kï·e] 'below' (< *kīḻe*). Such [ï] vowels are, however, predictable by ordered rules recapitulating the historical development; they remain descriptively distinct from the enunciative vowel, and there is no need to set up a basic *ï* for Irula.

5.9. In the Tamil dialect of the Kollimalai tribes, spoken in Salem District (Karunakaran 1971), [u] is described as occurring only in word-initial syllables, with [ï] everywhere else; thus we have [kuṛï] 'give' (p. 8).[8] In his morphophonemic section, Karunakaran has rules Ø → *u*, in a complex list of environments, and Ø → *i* / *y*____# (pp. 36, 38)—in effect generating the enunciative vowel both medially and finally. Lexical items are accordingly entered with final consonants, e.g. *āṭ-* 'goat'; however, basic final *u* is recognized in stems like *oru* 'one', *aru* 'cut'. This monograph deserves notice, then, as the only one I know of that consistently treats enunciative [ï] as predictable.

5.10. One other recent description of Tamil (mainly classical) is that of Andronov (1959). This author describes [u] as occurring in initial and medial syllables, finally in words like *teru* 'street', and also in the end of polysyllabic words with a sonant preceding the final *-u*: *kadavu* 'door', *ēẓu* 'seven' (pp. 13–14). Unrounded [ï] is said to occur in other final positions. Andronov continues (p. 14): 'There is a tendency in Modern Tamil to pronounce *ï* in some other cases too: *kadavu* and *kadavï* 'door' . . . *ēẓu* and *ēẓï* 'seven', etc.' This is the only report I have seen of rounded [u] in words of the patterns (C)VCVCV or (C)V̄CV.

6. The following data relate to certain other Tamil dialects spoken outside Tamil Nad proper.

6.1. The colloquial dialect of Jaffna, in Ceylon, as reported by Shanmugam Pillai (1962:96), shows enunciative *ï* in some instances, but contrastive *u* is also recorded: *udï* 'what one' (medium distance), *nanrru* 'good'. We may suppose that the dialect has fairly numerous cases of basic *u* in final position, but that consonant-final stems add enunciative [ï]. It is also claimed that this dialect has contrasting *ï* and *u* in initial syllables, e.g. *nïgam* '(finger) nail' vs. *nugam* 'yoke'. Since 'nail' is *nagam* in other dialects, it would appear that Jaffna has a rule raising *a* to *ï* in certain cases; but no further data are at hand to show us whether we must in fact recognize a basic vowel *ï*.[9]

6.2. With regard to the Sanketi Tamil dialect, spoken by a Brahmin group in Mysore State, Ananthanarayana (1968:7–8) indicates that the Kowsika dialect has final [u] after rounded stem vowels, and [ï] elsewhere. He gives examples such as: *puḷu* 'worm', *cundu* 'to blow the nose', as opposed to *kəḍï* 'to perish', *tappï* 'to err'. (The Bettadapura dialect has [i] rather than [ï]. Sanketi also shows a surface contrast between *u* and *ï*, since underlying *-am* yields Kowsika [u], e.g. *paḷḷam* > *paḷḷu* 'ditch' (compare *paḷḷm-ā* 'a ditch?'); less regularly, *-an* also yields [u], e.g. *akkan* > *akku* 'elder sister' (compare *akkn-ā* 'elder sister?').

In terms of our present framework, it seems quite possible to regard Kowsika [ï] as the automatic enunciative vowel throughout, with assimilation to [u] when a rounded vowel stands in the previous syllable. Final [u] elsewhere can be treated as basic /am an/.

6.3. The Tigala dialect of gardeners in Mysore State appears to have both [ï] and [u], unpredictably, in final position, e.g. *təppu* 'wrong' vs. *kappï* 'cup', *pillu* 'grass' vs. *kəllï* 'stone' (Cingaram 1968). It would be helpful to have some data on morphophonemic alternations, in order to decide whether *ï* and *u* must be set up as contrasting in the underlying structure.

6.4. Of two forms of Tamil reported from South Kanara (Shankar Bhat 1968b), the Padmasāle dialect generally shows enunciative [u] after rounded vowels or labials, as in the neighboring Tulu language (see §9 below); but exceptions appear, e.g. *buṭï* 'house' (vs. *būlu* 'fall').

On the other hand, the Kurvānï dialect shows [u] after labials, but [ï] after rounded vowels; furthermore, the enunciative vowel in this dialect becomes [i] not only after *y*, but after *l*—a phenomenon not noted elsewhere.

Malayalam

7.1. The enunciative vowel in Malayalam grammatical tradition and in modern speech has been discussed by Ramaswami Aiyar (1935:96–99), as follows:

The Malayalam sound *ï*, described as samvṛta (L [Līlātilakam], III, 1), besides occurring in all those positions in which the corresponding Tamil sound *ï* is found, is allowed as a final sound in Mal. in the following contexts:

(i) Optionally in connection with final *l, ḷ, n, ṇ,* and *r* . . . (except in intimate compounds) in instances like *kaṇṇï* (beside *kaṇ* 'eye' . . . in which the final *l, ḷ, n, ṇ* appear doubled after the short radical vowel of dissyllabic words, in instances like *viralï* (beside *viral* 'finger') . . . where the words have more than two syllables, and in words like *ārï* (besides *ār* 'who?') . . . with long basic vowels followed by short *l, r,* etc. [Footnote:] In the colloquial, the enunciative is embodied almost always (except in intimate compounds) before pauses and consonants in words like *kaṇṇï, kālï*. The pronouns *ñān, avan, avaḷ, avar* and the participial nouns involving the three last-mentioned forms do not generally embody *ï*. Original dissyllabic (and trisyllabic) words do not generally have *ï*.

It has to be observed that while Tamil grammars do not recognize the use in literary compositions of the final *ï* after *l, n, ḷ, ṇ, r* in the contexts (i.e., before consonants following) in which Mal. allows the use of the optional forms with final *ï*, forms like *kaṇṇï* (beside *kaṇ* 'eye'), *kālï* (beside *kāl* 'leg') . . . occur in the Tam. colloquial before pauses and before words with initial consonants. The Tamil grammars have not recognized this colloquial feature, while in Mal. recognition has been given to it by all grammars from the time of Līlātilakam. . . .

(ii) I have pointed out above that according to strict grammatical rules the final sound in Tam. *kadavu* (door), *puṟavu* (dove), etc. is *u* and not *ï*, though in vocalic sandhi the *u* here behaves like *ï* in that it is elided before a following vowel. In Mal., such words as *aḷavï* (measurement), *kaḷavï* (theft) are definitely recognized as having a final samvṛta *u*. . . .

Summing up, one may say that except in dissyllabic words like *maṟu* (wart), *naṭu* (middle), *kuru* (boil), *puḻu* (worm) in which a short basic vowel is followed by a single consonant, the final ukaram sound in Mal. (whenever and wherever it occurs) has always the value of a samvṛta, i.e., the value of *ï* in Mal.[10]

This samvṛta sound of Mal. is a more open and frontalized sound than the corresponding *ï* of Tamil. . . .

This Mal. *ï* is invariably elided before a following vowel within breath-groups and meaning groups in the colloquial and in modern prose, and in poetry within the pauses prescribed for verse-units.

To restate: the situation for classical Malayalam is essentially like that described above for classical Tamil (§4) with the following exceptions: (1) The colloquial tendency to use the enunciative after ALL consonants is given greater recognition in literary Malayalam; (2) the enunciative is always *ï*, even after *v*; (3) *ï* is phonetically not as far back as the corresponding Tamil sound.

7.2. For further data on modern standard Malayalam, I rely on my own observations. My informant, Mrs. Gomathi Hariharan of Trivandrum, a bilingual in Tamil, pronounces the Malayalam enunciative as a central vowel, different from her Tamil back [ï]. In Malayalam as in Tamil, the enunciative vowel normally appears after obstruents before nonvowels, e.g. *pāṭṭï* 'song', *anjï* 'five'. The vowel also occurs, in informal pronunciation, after sonorants, e.g. *mānï* 'deer', *pālï* 'milk'. After *y*, the vowel is even more fronted in my informant's pronunciation, but still phonetically distinct from *i*; e.g. *vāyï* 'mouth', *kayyï* 'hand'.

There are some surface contrasts of *ï* and *u* in pause-final environment: in past verb forms such as *kaṇḍu* 'saw' (compare *kaṇḍï* 'having seen'), and in a few nouns such as *pasu* 'cow'. As Ramaswami Aiyar (1927:7) notes, the Malayalam alphabet, until recent times, had only a single symbol for *ï* and *u*, but a new symbol was then invented to represent final *ï*. In terms of phonological analysis, we may take *ï* as the predictable vowel, corresponding to zero in underlying forms, whereas final *u* represents an underlying vowel: hence *kaṇ-t* (with appropriate rules for the consonants) yields *kaṇḍï* 'having seen', and *kaṇ-t-u* yields *kaṇḍu* 'saw'. However, Velayudhan (1973) notes that past tense *u* is often replaced by *ï* in answering questions: e.g. *kaṇḍō* 'Did you see?', *kaṇḍï* '(Yes,) I saw'. Malayalam also has proper names with final [u] (as in Tamil, cf. §5.6 above); Velayudhan points to contrasting *poṉṉï* 'gold', *poṉṉu* 'a man's name'; the dative case forms are *poṉṉ-iṉï* 'to gold', *poṉṉu-iṉï* 'to Ponnu', showing that the underlying stem forms are *poṉṉ* vs. *poṉṉu*.

In addition, *ï* is in surface contrast with zero in a common class of words, namely when it occurs as the dative case suffix: e.g. *avaṉ* 'he', *avaṉï* 'to him'; *kaviḷ* 'cheek', *kaviḷiṉ* 'of the cheek' (literary), *kaviliṉï* 'to the cheek' (cf. Venugopala Panikkar 1973). This is, of course, an important exception to the generalization that in Malayalam, and in Dravidian as a whole, *ï* is predictable. Rather than give up the generalization, however, I would prefer to say that dative *ï* is predictable if we consider not only the phonological environment, but also the grammatical environment: thus the suffix can be set up as basic *-(iṉ)u* with a rule *u* → *ï* in dative forms only.

The vowel *ï* also occurs in medial syllables, but there it tends to be shorter and less distinct. It apparently does not contrast with [u] in this position; my informant tends to use a weakly rounded vowel when there is a back rounded vowel in the preceding syllable, as in *mudïgï* 'back', but an unrounded vowel elsewhere. In morphological combinations, it is apparent that *ï* is inserted in certain consonant clusters, which I have not yet adequately defined; compare *ul̲-um* 'will plow' but *ul̲ï-du* 'plowed'.

7.3. The Pulaya dialect of Malalyalam, as spoken by a scheduled caste in the Trivandrum area, has been described by Subramoniam (1962:103) as having enunciative *ï* in all medial and final positions, freely alternating with rounded *u* 'after short vowel monosyllables'. Thus, where standard Malayalam always has an [u] suffix in finite past tense forms, the Pulaya dialect has forms like *araccï* 'she ground'. But with CVC stems, we have, e.g., *parï* or *paru* 'a boil'.

7.4. A dialect of Malayalam studied by G. K. Panikkar (reported by Subramonian 1973:55), is said to have enunciative [u] after vibrants, [i] after palatals and [ï] elsewhere. This is the only case I know of where vibrants condition the vowel quality.

7.5. A recent description of Cochin Malayalam phonemics (community unspecified) has been published by M. V. Sreedhar (1972). By this account (pp. 110–11), unrounded [ï] occurs after initial C*r*- (reflecting Skt. *r̥* in loanwords) and in a wide range of medial and final syllables; rounded [u] occurs in initial syllables, and finally in words like *pul̲u* 'worm'. Some word-medial occurrences of [u] are mentioned, but not clearly accounted for, e.g. [ul̲unnï] 'black gram', [kal̲ugan] 'vulture' (also transcribed as [kal̲ïgan]. Sreedhar calls *u* and *ï* separate phonemes, and gives the contrastive pairs /o:ḍu/ 'run!' vs. /o:dï/ 'tile' and /kal̲ugu/ 'wash!' vs. /kal̲ïgan/ 'vulture' (p. 101; but the latter word also appears as /kal̲ugan/ on p. 110). Examples elsewhere in the article consistently show final [u] in imperative verb forms (e.g. /iḍu/ 'put it!') as well in the past tense (e.g. /konnu/ 'killed').[11]

An analysis seems possible here, as for other dialects, in which [ï] is phonemically zero, whereas all occurrences of [u] reflect /u/. The striking feature of this Cochin data, however, is the apparent presence of /u/ as an imperative suffix.[12]

Mapila Malayalam

8. The most detailed information available to me at the moment about the *ï-u-Ø* alternation in South Dravidian is provided by Mrs. Suseela

P. Upadhyaya in her doctoral dissertation on Mapila Malayalam (1969), here abbreviated MM. The dialect she describes is that of a Muslim community living in South Kanara district, Mysore, among Tulu speakers; and it shows a striking degree of influence from Tulu in lexicon, grammar, and phonology.[13] The phonological patterns involving the enunciative vowel seem to be among the features specifically borrowed from Tulu; but in fact, thanks to Mrs. Upadhyaya's work, better documentation of these patterns is available for MM than for Tulu itself. The richness of the data warrants a detailed discussion here.

8.1. Mrs. Upadhyaya's description, in traditional structuralist terms, recognizes *ï* and *u* as distinct phonemes, and a large number of lexical items are established as ending in these units, e.g. *pālï* 'milk', *pandï* 'shake', *cāvu* 'death', *jappu* 'pound'. In her phonemic description, there is no comment on the distribution of these sounds relative to each other or to zero. However, an inspection of her lexicon suggests certain hypotheses about the occurrence of *ï* and *u* in non-initial syllables:

(1) *u* is especially frequent after a labial consonant, as in the examples above.

(2) *u* is also frequent when there is a rounded vowel in the preceding syllable, and this environment may be *u* itself in an initial syllable; e.g. *onnu* 'one', *mōnu* 'son', *nūru* 'hundred', *unnu* 'dine!'. The apparent assimilatory effect may spread from one syllable to the next, as in *uguru* 'nail'.

(3) *ï*, which never occurs in initial syllables, is found almost entirely in environments OTHER than those of labial consonants and rounded vowels, e.g. *īkïlï* 'broomstick', *kaḍalï* 'sea'.[14]

(4) Utterance-final *u* and *ï* are in almost complete complementary distribution with zero, since hardly any utterances are recorded as ending in consonants.[15]

(5) In utterance-final position after *y*, neither *u* nor *ï* occur, but *i* does occur, thus entering into the pattern of complementary distribution; e.g. *nāyi* 'dog', *koyi* 'reap'.[16]

Other lexical items attest a related set of facts: in loanwords, primarily of either Arabic or English origin, final *u* is added in the environments of labial consonants and rounded vowels, but *ï* is added otherwise; e.g. *islāmu* 'Islam', *ṭrippu* 'trip', *kānūnu* 'law' (Arabic *qānūn*), but *kurvānï* 'Koran', *ḍressï* 'dress'.

8.2. The relationship of MM *u, ï,* and Ø is more explicitly indicated in Mrs. Upadhyaya's sections on morphophonemics. There we learn of the following alternations (details of environment are omitted here):

(1) Both *ï* and *u* are said to be lost in certain environments: essentially, before vowels (p. 49),[17] or adjacent to sonorants (pp. 51–54, 79). Examples are *ōḍu* 'run!', *ōḍ-iye* 'I ran'; *kēkï* 'hear!', *kēk-re* 'I hear'.

(2) After *y,* the same kind of alternation applies to *i,* e.g. *koyi* 'reap!', *koy-ogu* (> *koyyogu*) 'for reaping', *koy-ḍe* 'I reap'.

(3) Certain morphological constructions show alternation of *u* and *ï*: 'The vowel *u* occurs when the preceding syllable contains a back vowel, and *ï* occurs when preceded by other vowels, provided there is no bilabial consonant or *y* is between the two vowels' (p. 55); e.g. *konn-e* 'I killed', *konnu* 'having killed', but *ninḍ-e* 'I stood', *ninḍï* 'having stood'. But *u* occurs after a bilabial consonant, e.g. *jappuḍe* 'I pound'—cf. *cellïḍe* 'I tell'. Furthermore, *i* appears after *y,* e.g. *pōy-e* 'I went', *pōyi* 'having gone' (p. 99).

8.3. It appears that the above alternations can be more economically accounted for by assuming that the vowels in question do not have phonologically basic status, but are predictable by rule. We can set up underlying forms such as *pāl* 'milk', *cāv* 'death', *koy* 'reap', *ōḍ* 'run', *japp* 'pound', *konn* 'having killed', and *pōy* 'having gone', on which something like the following rules operate:

$$\text{(1)}\quad \emptyset \rightarrow \text{ï} \;/\; \text{C}\_\_\_\_ \begin{Bmatrix} \text{pause} \\ \text{obstruent} \end{Bmatrix}$$

$$\text{(2)}\quad \text{ï} \rightarrow [\text{i}] \;/\; y\_\_\_\_$$

$$\text{(3)}\quad \text{ï} \rightarrow [\text{u}] \;/\; \begin{Bmatrix} \text{labial} \\ \text{rounded vowel} + \text{C(C)} \end{Bmatrix}\_\_\_\_$$

These rules operate within stems, as well as in morphological constructions. In environments other than those listed in 2 and 3, *ï* is of course phonetic [ï].

These rules have the advantage of permitting simpler basic forms, as well as simplifying the statement of phoneme distribution and morphophonemic alternation. There are, however, some items in the MM data that are not accounted for by such rules. These consist principally of cases of *u* in environments other than those of labial consonants and rounded vowels. Thus we find lexical items like *beru* 'wildcat', *kalu* 'vulture', *naḍu* 'hip'. We note, furthermore, that such items do not show loss of *u* before a vowel, but rather interpolating of *v*, parallel to interpolation of *y* after basic *i*: i.e. *naḍu-ā* > *naḍuvā* 'is it the hip?' is reminiscent of *katti* 'knife', *katti-ā* > *kattiyā* 'is it the knife?' We may conclude that *u* in such forms is not predictable, but represents a basic occurrence of the same short *u* phoneme found in initial syllables.[18]

Similarly, we find at least one suffixal element that has the shape -*u* regardless of environment, namely subjunctive 3 sing. masc.-neuter -*u* as in *piḍikk-u* 'he may catch' (historically, this is future -*um*). This vowel is never deleted, but does show interpolated *v* when another vowel follows: *piḍikkuv-e* 'I may hold', *piḍikkuv-a* 'we may hold' etc. (p. 71). An underlying *u* should again be recognized.

Some examples show [u] instead of expected [ï] in word-medial position, e.g. *irumbu* 'iron' (cf. *karïmbu* 'sugarcane'), *nakkulu* 'earthworm', *benuru* 'ash'. Such cases must be recognized as containing a rare basic medial *u*.

A few other forms in Mrs. Upadhyaya's thesis also raise analytical problems, and should be further investigated.[19] In general, however, we may say that MM has the basic vowels /i e a o u/, all occurring with contrastive length; that /u/ occurs, though rarely (like /o/), in noninitial syllables; that many morphemes end in basic consonants; that a regular rule adds the enunciative *ï* to such morphemes in certain environments; and that further rules govern assimilatory change of *ï* to *u* and to *i*.

Tulu

9. The existence of both [ï] and [u] as enunciative vowels in Tulu is relatively well known, being reflected in the Kannaḍa-based orthography that is used occasionally, and in the forms reproduced in Burrow and Emeneau's *Dravidian Etymological Dictionary* (1961). The vowels are described by Ramaswami Aiyar, who notes (1936:397, 438) that they appear not only after obstruents, but after all final consonants. He describes the relationship between them (pp. 435–38) as follows:

The vowels *i* and *u* as enunciatives:

(i) As in the other south Dravidian dialects, the vocalic enunciative at the end of old monosyllabic bases with short radical vowels and short terminal consonants is *-u*: *kaḍ-u* (hard, firm), *naḍ-u* (middle), *puru* (snail, worm), *ar-u* (brim, edge), etc.

(ii) Monosyllabic bases with long radical vowels or with short radical vowels followed by geminated consonants or by consonant groups, show generally (see below for exceptions) the enunciative *ï* in Tulu . . .: *nāḍ-ï* (country) . . . *kaṭṭ-ï* (bond) . . . *kaṇṇ-ï* (eye) . . . Dissyllabic bases also show *-ï*: *pudar-ï* (name) . . . *ugar-ï* (brackish) . . . *baraḍ-ï* (barren) . . .

(iii) Exceptions in Tulu to the above rule are furnished by instances where labial consonants or dorsal vowels in the neighbouring syllable are found; in all these cases the enunciative is *-u* and not *-ï*: *poṇṇ-u* (girl) . . . *bolp-u* (whiteness), *ucc-u* (kind of snake), *moroḍ-u* (empty), *kapp-u* (blackness).

(iv) Certain post-positional endings show *-ï*; the rule of vocalic harmony pointed out in (iii) above is applicable here too: *ari* (rice)—*ari-n-ï* (acc.), . . . *ūru* (country village)—*ūru-n-u* (Acc.) . . .

(vi) *-ï* or *-u* appears in the following conjugational forms; the rule of vocalic harmony is found here too: Third Person Sing. of the Present, the Past, the Perfect and the Pluperfect tenses: Compare Third Person Present Sing. *malp-uṇḍu* of the folk-speech and *ampuṇu* of the Brahmins' dialect, with the corresponding Past Sing. *maltïṇḍ-ï, antïṇ-ï*. . . .

Thus the Tulu situation seems to fit that described above for Mapila Malayalam. One qualification of Aiyar's statement is necessary: the final *u* in *kaḍu* 'hard' etc. should probably not be considered the enunciative vowel. Aiyar later refers to such examples as 'monosyllabic words' (p. 438, sec. g, note 1) and states that their final *u* is not 'elided in sandhi'; this seems to amount to saying that these words, like their counterparts in other Dravidian languages, are NOT monosyllabic, but have a basic second vowel *u*. Such an analysis is supported by Aiyar's discussion of Tulu in his 'Dravidic sandhi' paper (1935:109–10): 'There is a non-elidable final *-u* . . . in disyllabic forms with short radical vowels followed by a single consonant, as in *naḍu* (middle), *puḷu, puru* (worm) . . . When this *-u* meets another vowel, link-sounds [i.e. *v*] are produced.'

9.2. Turning to more recent descriptions, the data given for the Udupi Brahmin dialect by Shankar Bhat (1967) are typical for other dialects known to me from publications or from my own work with informants, and are again consistent with the Mapila Malayalam pattern. The vowel [ï] is short, with no long counterpart. It is very frequent finally—e.g. *maṇṇï* 'earth', *kaylï* 'ladle'—and medially—e.g. *battïnï* 'it came'. But it is rare in word-initial syllables, being found only in *rï* reflecting Sanskrit *r̥*. On the other hand, short [u] is common in initial syllables—e.g. *kuṇṭe* 'dwarf', *udaḷï* 'white ant', and not uncommon elsewhere—e.g. *uruḷu* 'noose', *pāpu* 'enough', *kukku* 'mango'. A minimal pair for surface [u] and [ï] is *aḷuve* 'mouth of a river' vs. *aḷïve* 'I weep' (Shankar Bhat, p. 14). But inspection of the data shows that the two sounds have a partially complementary distribution: In word-initial syllables, only [u] occurs (except after *r*, as noted above); in other positions [u] is found mainly when preceded by a labial consonant, directly or in a cluster—e.g. *avu* 'that', *pāpu* 'enough', *īmḷu* 'kind of leech'—or when there is a rounded vowel in the preceding syllable—e.g. *kukku* 'mango', *uruḷu* 'noose', *sōku* 'style'. In general, rules 1 and 3 given above in §8.3 seem to apply.

It is not clear whether enunciative [i] ever occurs after *y* in Tulu; negative evidence is Shankar Bhat's *kay* 'hand' (1967:27), *koy* 'pluck' (50), *kāy* 'to boil' (p. 77). But evidence for an enunciative *i* after *j* is provided by Ramaswami Aiyar (1935:109–10), who notes that '-*i* of *oñji* (one), *mūji* (three), *āji* (six) is elided before another following vowel: . . . *āj-ānæ* (six elephants) . . .' Other Dravidian languages have enunciative [ï] or [u] in these words; the fronting after *j* is apparently a development peculiar to Tulu.

Basic *u* in non-initial syllables occurs not only in CV̆CV forms, as mentioned by Ramaswami Aiyar, but occasionally elsewhere—finally, as in the plural suffix -*(k)ḷu* (*āṇi-ḷu* 'nails', *pili-kḷu* 'tigers', *ā-kḷu* 'they' (Shankar Bhat 1967:81) and the 3 sing. neuter subjunctive -*u* (*tintu* 'it might have eaten', p. 62); and medially, as in the present negative suffix -*uri* (*kaṭṭuri* 'does not tie', p. 56). Basic *u* must be recognized in such cases. Bhat's minimal pair for surface [u] and [ï], *aḷuve* 'river mouth' vs. *aḷïve* 'I weep' (p. 14), then reflects underlying *aḷuve* vs. *aḷ-ve*.

There is evidence that the Tulu enunciative is [u] rather than [ï] not only immediately after a labial, but also when another consonant intervenes; thus Bhat's data include *avṭu* 'out' (presumably from English) and *īmḷu* 'species of leech'. Again, it appears that enunciative [u] may be conditioned not only by a preceding rounded vowel but also by a following one, viz. final basic *u*; thus *kaṇṇï* 'eye' but *kaṇ-ṇuḷu* 'eyes', *ēḍï* 'goat' but *ēḍulu* 'goats' (Shankar Bhat 1967:81).

9.3. To summarize, we may say that Tulu follows the general Dravidian pattern regarding the enunciative vowel, with alternation of rounding according to the rules given above for Mapila Malayalam, and with a few minor peculiarities of its own. One other peculiarity needs mention: in the dialect described by Shankar Bhat (p. 40), there are 3 sing. neuter past forms like *sōjïnï* 'it wasn't seen' (stem *sōj-*) where the medial [ï] is not accounted for by any statements made so far. Since the occurrence of [ï] is otherwise so predictable, it seems advisable to treat such forms as exceptions, conditioned by the particular suffixal morpheme in question. Otherwise, *ï* may be omitted from the list of systematic phonemes for Tulu. Perhaps coincidentally, or perhaps not, the symbol for *ï* in the Kannada-based orthography for Tulu is that which, in Kannada, signals the ABSENCE of a vowel.

Kannada

10.1. The enunciative vowel is easily described for literary Kannada: it is rounded *u*. To quote Ramaswami Aiyar (1935:102–3),

> Final *-u* of all Kannada words except dissyllabic ones with short radical vowels followed by short consonants, like *naḍu* (middle), *puḻu* (*huḷu*) (worm), is elided when meeting other vowels: *nān-illi—nānu* (I) + *illi* (here) . . . but *puḻu-v-illa* (there is no worm) . . . etc., show that *-u* of *puḻu* . . . etc., is not elided.
>
> Practically, then, the difference in sandhi action between the non-elidable *-u* of dissyllabic words like *puḻu, naḍu,* and the elidable *-u* of other words corresponds to the difference (in vocalic sandhi) between the non-elidable Tam. muṟṟiyal-ukaram *u* and the elidable kuṟṟiyal-ukaram *ï*.
>
> The following points, however, are noteworthy: (i) There is no difference in the phonetic CHARACTER or value of the elidable *u* and the non-elidable *u* in Kannada; both have the same sound-value, viz., that of a rounded labial *u*. . . .

We may add some data and restate the facts in accordance with our general view of the Dravidian enunciative vowel: rather than speaking of a basic *-u* that is elided, we recognize that a large number of morphemes end in a basic consonant, e.g. *nāy* 'dog', *nān* 'I', *māḍ* 'do'. When something other than a vowel follows, the enunciative must appear; after *y* it is *i*, e.g. *nāyi* 'dog'; elsewhere it is always rounded *u*, e.g. *nānu* 'I', *māḍu* 'do' (Bright 1958a:13, §2.2, and 1970, rule 8). A small number of morphemes end in basic *u*, e.g. *huḷu* 'worm', *magu* 'child'. These basic vowels are stable; when they are followed by another vowel, they are not elided, but a semivowel is interposed, e.g. *maguv-ina* 'of a child' (Bright 1958a:17, §2.9, and 1970, rule 10).

10.2. In colloquial Kannada as spoken in Mysore city or Bangalore, the same rules operate, except that in word-medial position the enunciative vowel may be a very brief [ï] (Ramanujan 1963:262); e.g. **māḍ-tt-āne* 'he does' > lit. *māḍu-tt-āne* > colloq. *māḍïttāne*. In more rapid speech this [ï] may be lost, like other short vowels (Bright 1970, rule 13), thus *māḍtane*. A vowel [ï] may also be heard in Sanskrit loanwords like *rïtu* (or *rutu*) 'season' (Bright 1970, rule 3, and cf. §3.3 above), and sporadically before retroflexes, especially in forms of *bïḍu* (< *biḍu*) 'leave it !'.

10.3. By contrast with the above, several reports on dialectal Kannada provide evidence for more frequent vowels of the [ï] type, as follows.

In the Sholiga dialect, spoken by a tribal group of the Biligiri-Rangan hills, /i ī e ē/ 'have strongly retroflexed central unrounded allophones occurring before retroflex consonants, providing (a) they are preceded by an initial velar stop, or (b) the retroflex consonant is followed by a high vowel, or (c) both' (Gurubasave Gowda 1968:13). The pattern seems to resemble that of the geographically proximate Koḍagu language (see §11 below). The enunciative vowel, however, is [u].

In the Kannada dialect of Sivalli Brahmins in Barkur, South Kanara (Acharya 1969a), the enunciative vowel seems to be normally [ï], but underlying final *u* is pronounced in forms like *hasu* 'cow', *koḍu* 'it may give'. The phonological pattern thus seems more like that of Malayalam (see §7.1, above) than that of other Kannada dialects.

In the Kōṭa Brahmin dialect, near Mangalore (Navada 1970), the enunciative *ï* often appears in final and medial syllables (e.g. *kodï* 'give!', *hōtïlï* 'she goes'), but contrastive *u* is common (e.g. *koḍu* 'it may give', *maḍu* 'axe', *beduru* 'bamboo', *dāṇṭu* 'cross'). Presumably we must recognize basic *u* as relatively common in non-initial syllables, contrasting with the basic zero, which gives rise to enunciative [ï]. Data on morphophonemic alternations are needed in order to reach a proper phonological analysis.

In the Kannada spoken by weavers in Chinnalpatti, Madurai District, the enunciative vowel is presented as /u/, with a [ï] allophone 'in the non-initial syllables except when preceded by *u*' (R. Mahadevan 1968a:13). The Kannada dialect used by Kurubas in Coimbatore District similarly has enunciative *u,* which is 'unrounded in non-initial syllables, provided it is not preceded by the vowels *u* or *o*' (R. Mahadevan 1968b:15). These dialects, spoken in Tamil territory, may be seen as showing influence of one common Tamil pattern.

In the northern Kannada area, several dialects are reported to have replaced some cases of final *u* with [ə], coinciding phonetically with the metaphonic [ə] < *a* in initial syllables (data from U. P. Upadhyaya [1968, 1969] on Gulbarga and Bidar dialects, and from Acharya [1968] on Rabakavi Kannada and Bijapur District). We seem to be dealing here with an enunciative vowel that has been lowered from [ï] to [ə], but it is not clear whether the relative distribution of [ə] and [u] is describable in purely phonological terms.

The dialect of Tiptur, in Tumkur District, is described (Acharya 1969b) as having a vowel of the [ï] type in occasional contrast with [u], but details are not available. It appears that the enunciative vowel is always [u] in final syllables, but occasionally [ï] when medial.

Kodagu

11. The following information on the descriptive and historical status of the Kodagu (Coorg) vowels is drawn from Emeneau (1970). The language has two back unrounded phones, high *ï* and mid *ë*. In initial syllables, these are regular developments of earlier *i e* before retroflexes, as in *gïṇi* 'parrot' (Ka. *giṇi*); this backing of vowels is parallel to that described above for several varieties of Tamil.[20] In non-initial syllables, however, *ï* represents the regular enunciative vowel for Kodagu, e.g. *tītï* 'feed!'. After *v, u* is regular (e.g. *cāvu* 'corpse'; with an exception, compare Emeneau 1970:151.) But contrastive final [u] occurs in the 'potential' suffix *-u* (from earlier *-um,* e.g. *taku* 'may give' as compared with *takï* 'language') and in words like *maḷu* 'chili' (compare Tamil *miḷaku*), *taḍu* 'delay' (compare Tamil *taḍavu*), *puḷu* 'worm' (compare Tamil *puḻu*). The history of such forms is discussed by Emeneau (p. 147). Descriptively, it appears that, as in many Tamil dialects, we have here occasional cases of basic *u* outside initial syllables. Final [ï] then reflects, as in the other languages generally, underlying zero.[21]

Telugu

12. Like standard Kannada, Telugu appears to have to have rounded [u] wherever the general Dravidian pattern requires an enunciative vowel. To quote Ramaswami Aiyar (1935:105–6),

> In vocalic junction, the final *-u* of all Telugu words and forms is elided before another vowel. . . .
>
> *-u* in final positions of Telugu words appears in the literary dialect after all consonants except after the consonantal druta *n* in certain contexts and after *l* and *r* in the oldest literary texts and inscriptions; in the colloquial, this *-u* appears (with greater or lesser distinctness) after all consonants in final positions, except *-m-*.
>
> The distinction observed in Tamil between muṟṟiyal-ukaram and kuṟṟiyal-ukaram sounds does not exist in Telugu either in respect of the sound-value or in respect of the behaviour in sandhi contexts, since (for historical reasons) vocalic sandhi contexts involving purely dissyllabic words with short vowels and consonants (similar to those in which Tam. has muṟṟiyal-ukaram) ceased to exist in the pre-literary period.

I have not seen any data on Telugu dialects to indicate departure from the above statements.

Other Dravidian Languages

13. A number of other languages, spoken by tribal peoples, may be briefly surveyed by way of comparison with the findings reported above.

13.1. In Kuruba, as spoken by the Beṭṭa Kurubas of Coorg District, Mysore (U. P. Upadhyaya 1972), long and short /i/ takes on [ï] quality in the environment followed by a retroflex or *r*—i.e., after the pattern of Kodagu. After labials, [ï] develops further to [u]. The enunciative vowel is regularly [ï].

13.2. In Erukula (Korchi, Korava), spoken in Andhra Pradesh, the enunciative vowel is apparently /u/, described as having an allophone [ï] 'in the word-final position when front vowels occur in the preceding syllable' (Gurreddy 1968:1).

However, the dialect described by Srinivasavarma (1969) seems to show a different distribution: enunciative *ï* is regularly recorded when final (e.g. *pellï* 'tooth', *ōgï* 'seven'), and occasionally when medial (e.g. *nikkïdï* 'it stands'); rounded *u* regularly appears finally after *u ū* (e.g. *igisu* 'unload', *jiguru* 'trap'). For this latter dialect, at least, it seems that we must recognize basic *u* as occurring rather often in non-initial syllables, contrasting there with the basic zero, from which the enunciative [ï] may arise.

13.3. Belari, spoken in South Kanara, appears to have enunciative [ï] and [u] distributed much as in the neighboring Tulu (Shankar Bhat 1968a).

13.4. Koraga, also spoken in South Kanara, shows some features that suggest Northern Dravidian ties. Information has been published by Shankar Bhat on three forms of the language. The Onti dialect seems for the most part to have enunciative [ï] and [u] distributed as in Tulu, but with occasional exceptions like *geddu* 'to win' (1968c:7.10). Morphophonemic alternations of *ï, u,* and Ø are attested, however (1968c: 7.16, 8.9), following Tulu-type rules. The Mudu dialect, in the examples available (1968f) shows [ï] and [u] distributed as in Tulu. The Tappu dialect (1968e) seems to show a greater independence of the two sounds: the enunciative vowel is usually [ï], but also appears as [u] in unexpected positions, and there are examples like *nēvu* 'fear' vs. *nāvï* 'to get up'.

13.5. As regards the enunciative vowel in other tribal languages, we may refer to Emeneau (1970:153), who states:

> Comparison of the various languages shows that it occurs in . . . Koṇḍa, Kui-Kuwi, and Malto. It does not occur in Toda-Kota (the absence here apparently resulting from the general loss in these two languages of short vowels, except *i,* in non-initial syllables), the Kolami-Parji group (with exceptional occurrence in one dialect of Gadba), Gondi (except in one dialect), Pengo-Manḍa, Kurukh, and Brahui.

In a personal communiation, Emeneau points out that this statement should be qualified as regards Parji: Burrow and Bhattacharya (1953:2) report sporadic 'auxiliary *u*' in that language.

Conclusion

14. Considering the data presented above, we may sum up in terms of the following generalizations, which are intended to have both synchronic and diachronic relevance.

14.1. Dravidian has always had morphemes ending in one or two consonants, e.g. *kāṭ* 'forest', *teṅk* 'coconut tree', and in vowels, including *u*. Originally, stems with final *-u* were mostly of the shape CVC*u*, e.g. *pul̠u* 'worm'.

14.2. From an early period, a phonological rule has operated in most languages that adds a vowel after most consonants when a consonant or pause follows. The rule is most widely attested in the Southern Dravidian languages; its spread elsewhere is likely to be due to diffusion rather than to genetic transmission.

14.3. The consonants after which this enunciative vowel occurs were, in the oldest records, mainly the obstruents; but in modern dialects they tend to occur after any consonant.

14.4. The quality of the enunciative vowel is basically nonfront, nonlow, and unrounded; we may use the cover symbol *ï*. In a variety of dialects, it is fronted to [i] after *y*, and/or backed to [u] after rounded vowels and labial consonants. Diffusion of rules across genetic boundaries seems to have played an important role here. Some Central Dravidian languages have [i] after consonant clusters; and the Bettadapura dialect of Sanketi Tamil regularly has [i] even after single consonants.

14.5. In Kannada and Telugu, at least in the literary dialects and in most of the colloquial dialects reported, the enunciative vowel has in general become [u], merging phonetically with original or underlying *u*.

14.6. In medial syllables, the enunciative vowel often appears by the same general rule that generates it in final position, e.g. between stem and consonantal suffix (as in lit. Kannada *kāḍu-gaḷu* 'forests'). However, data are lacking for an exact statement.

14.7. In Tamil, original *u* in non-initial syllables, contrasting in the underlying structure with the zero that yields the enunciative [ï], has tended to merge phonetically with [ï] in some dialects; thus *naṭu* 'middle' often is pronounced [naḍï]. The rounded quality is most stable when a rounded vowel precedes, e.g. in *uḍu* 'wear'.

14.8. In a number of Tamil dialects and in Kodagu, front vowels of initial syllables are retracted before retroflex consonants; in some cases this results in phonetic merger, where *i* > *ï*, pronounced like the enunciative vowel. In general, however, the two different sources of [ï] remain descriptively distinguishable; there seems no need to set up *ï* as a basic phonological unit.

14.9. In a few scattered instances, the data suggest that *ï* may be coming into contrast both with zero and with basic *u*, and thus acquiring the status of a distinct systematic phoneme (see §§6.1, 6.3, 7.2, 9.3). In all these instances, more descriptive data would be welcome. In any case, the generalization still holds: Dravidian [ï] is usually not basic, but predictable by rule.[22]

NOTES

1. The vowel in question ranges in articulation from central to back, with both close and open variants; but it is always nonfront, nonlow, and unrounded. It is transcribed by various authors with the barred *i*, the shwa, or the turned *m;* throughout the present paper, however, *ï* is used as cover symbol.

2. From this point onward, the symbols *ï* and *u* are used to distinguish nonfront unrounded and rounded vowels respectively, and quoted material is retranscribed in accordance with this usage. Quoted material is also normalized in other ways; e.g. the retroflex glide appears everywhere as *ḻ*. In examples from literary Tamil-Malayalam (and in morphophonemic notation) I follow usual practice in transcribing medial *k c ṭ t p* as such; but in examples from the colloquial dialects, I use symbols that more closely represent the voiced and/or fricative pronunciation—thus lit. Ta. *teṅkï* 'coconut tree', colloq. *teṅgï*.

3. This statement applies essentially to monosyllables. In longer words, as pointed out by Marr and Kothandaraman (1973), many varieties of colloquial Tamil drop final /n m/ (with nasalization of preceding vowel) and /y l ḷ/: thus we have *vantāṉ* 'he came', colloq. *vandā̃; mānkāy* 'mango', colloq. *māngā̃; kantal* 'rag', colloq. *kandā̃*. I have suggested (Bright 1973) that colloquial Tamil requires a sequence of ordered rules such as the following:

(1) $V \rightarrow \tilde{V}$ / ____N#
(2) Sonorant → Ø / V____# (with restrictions depending on dialect)
(3) C → Cï / ____#

4. '(Vowel or) vowel-consonant' is here the translator's clumsy way of referring to the 'letter' or akṣara, i.e. the (C)V sequence.

5. As pointed out by Subramoniam (1973), there are alternative forms such as *naṭu, naṭuvu* 'middle' and *puḻu, puḻuvu* 'worm'. We may account for these

facts by setting up basic forms like *naṭuv, puḻuv;* then there is an optional rule *uv* → [u] when word-final. Whenever the optional rule is not applied, the enunciative vowel is added in the normal way.

6. Bh. Krishnamurti (in a personal communiation) gives the following historical account of how the *u*/zero contrast functions in derivational morphology: 'Given a root like *waṯ,* if the derivative vowel /u/ follows we have **waṯ-u* = Ta. *vaṟu* ['parch'] (DED 4355); if no vowel follows, the S. Dr. forms are Ta. Ma. *vaṟṟu* ['dry up'] etc. When a stem like C_1VC_2 (where C_2 = obstruent) is a whole utterance or enters inflection, it becomes C_1VC_2 (C_2u), where C_2u are predictable.'

7. Shanmugam Pillai (1956) interprets Tolkāppiyam (Moḻimarapu, p. 35) as reporting a minimal contrast in Old Tamil between final [ï] and [u], such that noun forms end in [ï] but verbal imperatives in rounded [u], e.g. [kaṭṭï] 'a bundle' vs. [kaṭṭu] 'bundle (it)! tie (it)!'. If this is valid, we might hypothesize that the Old Tamil imperative was formed with an overt suffix, phonologically a basic rounded *u*; but modern Tamil, with most other Dravidian languages, uses the unsuffixed stem as the singular imperative, with the enunciative vowel then automatically added.

8. This is, coincidentally, the pattern also described for spoken literary Tamil by Rajaram (1972).

9. In the same paragraph, Shanmugam reports similar contrasts in Indian colloquial Tamil: *vïrïpï* 'desire' and *tïrïpï* 'turn' vs. *turïpï* 'army'. The first two words correspond to lit. Ta. *virïppï* 'desire', *tirïppï* 'turn'; this suggests that there is a rule backing *i* to *ï* when there is an *ï* in the next syllable. But I have found no data elsewhere bearing on this matter.

10. Ramaswami Aiyar perhaps overlooks here a fact he had noted elsewhere (1927:7), namely that final [u] also occurs in past tense verb forms like *kaṇḍu* 'saw'; see §7.2 below. But there seem to be Malayalam dialects that have [ï] even in such forms; compare §7.3.

11. The same pattern appears in the description of Malayalam (locality unspecified) by Syamala Kumari (1972).

12. This is reminiscent of Shanmugam Pillai's suggestion (1956) regarding Old Tamil; compare footnote 7, above.

13. The Mapila community also exists, of course, in Kerala itself, but no information is available to me on the dialect spoken there. For present purposes, 'MM' refers only to the dialect spoken in South Kanara.

14. Velayudhan (1973) refers to dialects that also have forms like *māṉu* 'deer', *maṇṇu* 'earth', where the occurrence of final *u* (rather than standard *ï*) seems unpredictable. It would be important to know what happens when the interrogative enclitic is added to such forms. Does 'Is it a deer?' come out as *māṉuvō*? If so, we must recognize that etymological *māṉ* has been restructured in these dialects to basic *māṉu*. Or is the result *māṉō*? If so, then presumably

the basic form is still *mā<u>n</u>*, and we must reluctantly recognize a rule that prescribes enunciative *u* rather than *ï* for a particular list of morphemes.

15. Exceptions in Mrs. Upadhyaya's lexicon include *innum* 'still more', *paylmān* 'wrestler', and *vāpas* 'back'.

16. Final *i* is not recorded in certain monosyllabic nouns with short vowels, e.g. *kay* 'hand', *key* 'paddy plant'; but compare *neyi* 'ghee', *mayi* 'collyrium'.

17. The rule is stated by Mrs. Upadhyaya as applying to short vowels in general, but only one out of the ten examples involves a vowel other than *u* or *ï*. It is not clear how general the application of the rule should actually be.

18. Velayudhan (1973) points out that, in other varieties of Malayalam, words of this type vary with longer forms, e.g. *beru* or *berugï* 'wildcat', *naḍu* or *naḍuvu* 'hip'. For such varieties, we may set up basic *berug, naḍuv,* with a rule that optionally deletes *g* and *v* in the environment before *u#* (compare the Tamil case described in note 5, supra).

19. A troublesome form is *udïrï* '(hair, leaves) fall'.

20. On this parallelism, Emeneau (1970:153) comments: 'I have published a similar observation for Kolami, and have field-notes on the subject for several of the languages which I recorded.'

21. Emeneau (1970:153) suggests that the split of the enunciative vowel into two phones [u] and [ï], as shared with Tamil and Malayalam, 'may be taken to be an innovation in South Dravidian minus Kannada'. He continues (footnote 7), 'This type of distribution is seen for other features beside this one; it leads to splitting South Dravidian into Kannada as opposed to the rest of the SDr. languages . . .' But as we have seen, the phonetic distinction of [u] and [ï] occurs in some Kannada dialects, as well as in Tulu, which is not at all clearly classifiable as a South Dravidian language. It is perhaps preferable to think of the vowel pattern in question as an areal feature, rather than one corresponding to a genetic subgrouping.

22. In his *Comparative Dravidian phonology,* Zvelebil (1970:53–55) discusses the development of the enunciative vowel, which he refers to as 'nonmorphemic . . . obligatory and therefore fully predictable . . .' However, he then follows the structuralist tradition of taxonomic phonemics; thus he describes Old Tamil enunciative [ï] as an allophone of /u/, but says that in Malayalam [ï] 'has achieved true PHONEMIC status' because of its surface contrast with [u].

The difference between structuralist and generative approaches is well illustrated in Zvelebil's footnote 14 (p. 53). Discussing Koḍagu [ï] (compare §11 in the present paper), he distinguishes final [u] and [ï] as separate phonemes in examples like [naḍu] 'middle' vs. [naḍï] 'plant it'. He then writes:

> It is true that the occurrence of *-ï* seems to be wholly predictable in terms of morphological conditioning. Therefore, argues A. K. Ramanujan (personal communication), one should posit here a contrast of *naḍu* 'middle' n.: *naḍ* 'plant'

> v., and do away entirely with the opposition *u* : *ï*, denying phonemic status to -*ï*. It is all a matter of approach. We [i.e. Zvelebil] feel that, with the Koḍ. native speaker, the contrast between -*u* : -*ï* is very real. . . .

To be sure, but one may argue, in support of Ramanujan, that the basic reality is not the superficial phonetic difference, but rather the difference between the presence of a vowel *u* vs. the absence of any distinctive vowel at all.

9

How Not To Decipher the Indus Valley Inscriptions

One of the great unsolved problems of Indian history is the decipherment of the inscriptions from the ancient civilizations of the Indus Valley. The topic has been of special interest to Dravidianists because there seem to be two good arguments for the hypothesis that the Indus Valley language was an early form of Dravidian: first, the presence in modern times of Brahui, a Dravidian language, in Baluchistan, just west of the Indus Valley; and second, the fact that lexical and phonological loans from Dravidian existed in the earliest forms of Sanskrit, presumably reflecting language contact at the time when Indo-Aryan speakers first entered the Indian subcontinent by way of the Indus Valley. However, conclusive proof for this position has not yet been found, and alternative hypotheses continue to be put forward. The two principal types of suggestion are that the Indus Valley language was (a) a language otherwise known from the area of Mesopotamia, e.g., Sumerian; or (b) an early variety of Indo-Aryan, i.e., either Sanskrit itself or a dialect akin to Sanskrit. The latter type of hypothesis is supported in a recent book by the British Sanskritist John Mitchiner (1981). The book deserves the careful attention of everyone interested in the Indus Valley civilization. I believe, however, that Mitchiner fails to make his case, because of both linguistic and logical flaws in his argument.

In Chapter 1, 'The study of the Indus script' (pp. 1–18), Mitchiner reviews the literature on the topic and points to several important controversies. For instance, scholars in Finland (Parpola et al. 1968, 1969, 1970), as well as in the Soviet Union (Knorozov et al. 1972) and the United States (Fairservis 1975) have suggested that the Indus script was principally 'logographic', i.e., that the symbols corresponded mainly to lexical units such as words or morphemes. But Mitchiner rather summarily rejects this view (p. 4) and lays the basis for his own eventual conclusions by proposing that the symbols were primarily syllabic, i.e., that they represented particular consonant-vowel sequences (p. 12). Yet, as we see in later chapters, Mitchiner does interpret some symbols lexically. He further discusses the possibility of a historical continuity between the Indus Valley script and the later Brahmi script, and with rather brief discussion concludes that the two scripts 'may be directly related to each other' (p. 12); this belief recurs in much stronger form as Mitchiner proceeds. Finally, he notes that 'at least some of the Indus seals were attached to bales of merchandise' (p. 16); and from this he produces a hypothesis, on which he later relies heavily, that 'at least some of the inscriptions . . . refer to the type or quantity of the merchandise . . . or the name of the place whence the merchandise originates, or whither it is to be delivered' (p. 17). This is the basis for subsequent chapters in which Mitchiner attempts to identify 'two categories of placenames . . . referring on the one hand to places within the Indus Civilization, and on the other hand to its trading partners in the Persian Gulf and Sumer' (ibid.). Although he believes that the Indus seals were important in trade across the Arabian Sea, Mitchiner does not explain why the seals are in fact so much more numerous in the Indus Valley than in the Persian Gulf.

Chapter 2, 'The Seven High Places' (pp. 19–33), is based on a suggestion by Bailey (1975) that 'the archaic Ṛg Veda phrase *sápta síndhavas* and the Avesta phrase *hapta hindu* may have originally meant "The Seven High Places",' and that there is a Sumerian phrase *bàd imin* meaning 'The Seven Enclosed Places', used for a land to the east (p. 19). On this rather slight foundation, Mitchiner reasons as follows:

(a) The Indus symbol probably means 'seven'.

(b) It frequently occurs in the two combinations 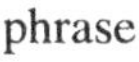 and 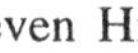.

(c) The sign has some similarity to the Sumerian sign , meaning 'city'.

(d) The Indus sign has some similarity to Sumerian 'mountain'.

(e) Therefore IF the Indus Civilization used a phrase 'Seven High

Places' to refer to itself, then (collapsing the semantic notions of 'city', 'high place', and 'mountain') that phrase corresponds to the Indus sign-groups  and  (p. 28).

Mitchiner's tendency to construct arguments like this, by piling one tenuous suggestion or assumption on top of another, is made especially clear by his frequent use of expressions such as 'It would therefore seem quite plausible . . . ,' 'It may be deemed as likely . . . .,' and 'One may perhaps infer. . . .' (pp. 27–28). But apart from this, it is extraordinary that, in two supposedly synonymous sign-groups, the number 'seven' should be the first element of one, but the second element of the other. In terms of general linguistic experience, it would be extremely unlikely to find a language which placed numerals invariably after one noun, but before another.

Mitchiner then considers a common sign-group,  , found especially at Mohenjo Daro. He likens the sign  with Sumerian  , meaning 'shrine' or 'throne', and thus interprets 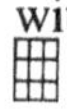 as meaning 'throne' or 'king' (p. 30). He then takes up the Indus sign  , which seems to occur (following the general belief that writing was from right to left) only in suffixal position. On the basis of correlations with Dravidian, this sign was associated by Parpola et al. with the genitive singular case; since Mitchiner rejects Dravidian connections, it is surprising to find him saying that 'It may be accepted as a working hypothesis' that the genitive identification is correct (p. 31). Mitchiner then points to the fact that the sign-group  is especially common at Mohenjo Daro, and he proposes that in fact it means 'from or of Mohenjo Daro', with the literal meaning 'of the high place of the king'; and he compares this with Sanskrit placenames like *Rājagiri* (p. 32). But in the Indus script, the symbol  , which Mitchiner translates as 'king', i.e., the modifying element, FOLLOWS (in the right-to-left order) the symbol  , supposedly meaning 'high place', i.e., the nuclear element. This order is contrary to the grammatical patterns of both Indo-Aryan and Dravidian language families, since both of these place a modifier BEFORE a nucleus.

At the end of Chapter 2, Mitchiner notes that a sign-group which immediately precedes  'will represent a nominal form'; but he then leaps to a non-sequitur by adding, 'that is to say, some kind of proper name' (p. 33). He repeats this elsewhere in the book (pp. 45, 51, 62). But why, we may ask, must all nouns in the Indus inscriptions be proper names? And Mitchiner goes even farther: such a noun 'is likely to denote a purely personal name'—and, again piling assumptions upon assumptions, he concludes that inscriptions containing  are likely to 'denote the region or town from which there originates that to which the rest of the inscription may refer' (pp. 32–33). A question not considered by Mitchiner is this: if 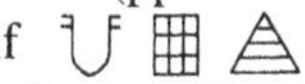 means 'from Mohenjo Daro', why is it found principally AT Mohenjo Daro? One gets an unlikely picture of the Mohenjo Daro merchants, baling and sealing their merchandise, but then finding no place to send it.

In Chapter 3, 'Categories of sign-groups (1)' (pp. 34–46), Mitchiner gives a useful catalogue of signs and sign-groups found to precede , and focuses on five which seem especially important. Then he resumes his usual style of argument: 'Since it has been seen [!] in Chapter 2 that several . . . sign-groups which . . . also appear preceding terminal  . . . represent the names of towns or regions, IT MAY BE DEEMED LIKELY that the same is the case with the five sign-groups just isolated' (p. 45, emphasis supplied). The commonest sign-group of this set is 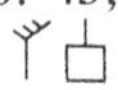, appearing mainly at Harappa; and Mitchiner proposes that this is in fact the name of Harappa (p. 46). Again, there is no explanation why goods marked as FROM a city should remain IN that city.

Chapter 4, 'Categories of sign-groups (2)' (pp. 47–52) introduces another apparently suffixal sign, , which is found to be mutually exclusive with , in terms of the sign-groups which they follow. From this Mitchiner concludes, surprisingly, that the two signs must 'perform different tasks in the script . . . [they] could not . . . represent different suffixes denoting the same case' (p. 47). But this seems to go against all linguistic experience. For instance, the fact that the Tamil suffix *-kaḷ* occurs with certain nouns, e.g., *peṇ* 'woman', but that the suffix *-aar* occurs with other nouns, e.g., *taay* 'mother', is part of the reason that we see *-kaḷ* and *-aar* as alternative forms of the plural suffix, rather than two contrasting suffixes. Nevertheless, Mitchiner adopts the suggestion of Parpola et al. that the sign  marks the dative case—in spite of the fact that the Finnish analysis is part of a Dravidian hypothesis which Mitchiner rejects. A list of sign-groups occurring with  is then given, and Mitchiner proposes (p. 51) that these represent another set of place names—rather improbably, the names of places which things are always sent TO, but never sent FROM.

Chapter 5, 'Categories of sign-groups (3)' (pp. 53–59), lists sign-groups used independently of the suffixal signs  and  . Mitchiner attempts few conclusions from this material.

Chapter 6 'Dilmun, Magan and Meluhha' (pp. 60–65) summarizes the foregoing analysis, moving from 'almost certainly' and 'most probably' to 'consequently' and 'therefore' (p. 62). Mitchiner says that 'the name of the place WHENCE the merchandise . . . originates or WHITHER it is to be delivered . . . will refer ON THE ONE HAND to places within the Indus Civilisation, and ON THE OTHER HAND to the Indus trading-partners in the Persian Gulf' (p. 63, emphasis supplied); this, of course, makes no allowance for trading WITHIN the Indus Valley. However, Mitchiner concludes further that a three-sign group followed by 'genitive'  'would seem likely to represent such a trisyllabic name as Meluhha'—a Sumerian name which has been linked to Sanskrit *mleccha,* referring to the non-Aryan peoples of India. Similarly, when two-sign groups are followed by 'dative' , Mitchiner feels that 'it is by no means inconceivable' that these correspond to Persian Gulf place names such as Dilmun, Magan, and Sumer (pp. 64–65). He even offers some similarities between Indus and Brahmi signs to support his analysis, but adds: 'It must regrettably be admitted . . . that we are here entering the realm of speculation' (p. 65).

Chapter 7, 'The grammatical forms of the inscriptions' (pp. 66–67) begins by examining other terminal signs which are possibly to be analysed as affixes of case and/or number. Again, some of Mitchiner's arguments are linguistically suspect. Thus the sign  was thought by Parpola et al. to mark the nominative plural; but Mitchiner points out that it is sometimes preceded by 'genitive singular'  . Could it be somehow redundant with  ? Mitchiner points out that  occurs frequently after multiple sign-groups, which he apparently takes to represent coördinate constructions; from this he concludes that  marks the genitive PLURAL (p. 68). But it would be extremely unusual for a language to mark the plurality of a coördinate phrase by adding a plural marker to the second member only: we cannot render 'mother and father' as 'mother-father-plural'. From here, Mitchiner moves to a comparison of his supposed Indus 'suffixes' with certain signs in the Brahmi syllabary. The argument takes this form: Indus  is 'comparable' to Brahmi  , pronounced *sa*; therefore Indus  is equated with the genitive suffixes *-as* of Sanskrit and *-sa* of Prakrit (pp. 73–75). It is thus concluded that the language of the Indus inscriptions 'may very well be' an early form of Indo-Aryan (p. 77). For the reasons expressed above, I feel that, equally, the language in question 'may very well be' something else altogether. The structure of Mitchiner's arguments is simply too shaky to support his conclusions.

As I have urged elsewhere (Bright 1986), greater care in both linguistic and logical treatment will be needed before we can make real progress in the decipherment of the Indus Valley script. Of the current research with which I am acquainted, I can point to the meticulous and cautious work of Iravatham Mahadevan (e.g., 1986) as especially likely to produce results of lasting value.

10

Archaeology, Linguistics, and Ancient Dravidian

The hypothesis that a Dravidian language was spoken by the Ancient Indus Valley civilization of Mohenjo-Daro and Harappa has long been considered highly plausible, and on several grounds. First, the presence of a modern Dravidian language in the hills to the west of the Indus, namely Brahui, is most easily explained if the Brahui are seen as the linguistic descendants of the ancient Indus Valley people. Second, the identification of Dravidian loan words in the Sanskrit of the earliest Vedic texts, by Emeneau and others, indicates that the first contacts between Sanskrit and Dravidian must have occurred when Sanskrit speakers first entered the Indian Subcontinent, i.e., when they arrived in the Indus Valley. Finally, evidence for a Dravidian substratum in many modern Indo-Aryan languages suggests that Dravidian languages once had wide distribution in the northern part of the subcontinent. But if the identification of the Indus Valley language as Dravidian is accepted, many questions still remain, for example: With what other languages was Dravidian in contact, and where, and when? What was the cultural nature of the contact? And what chronology can be assigned to cultural and linguistic shifts in the ancient Indus Valley and adjacent areas?

The eminent archaeologist Dr. Walter A. Fairservis, Jr., author of an authoritative text on Indian prehistory (1975), has recently attempted to offer answers to such questions, in a paper entitled 'The consequences of Harappan as a Dravidian language'. His method is to present six 'axioms' regarding the relationship between archaeology and linguistics, each of which has this general form: 'If one finds certain types of cultural assemblages, i.e. collections of material-culture items as recovered by archaeology, then one can infer certain facts about the corresponding languages.' Applying these axioms to data from the Indus Valley, Fairservis derives a rather detailed ethnolinguistic prehistory of the area.

I welcome such attempts to coordinate research in linguistics and archaeology; earlier attempts to relate these two fields, in other parts of the world, have been made in recent years by myself (cf. Bright and Bright 1976), and by other scholars (Ehret 1976, Kinkade and Powell 1976). If a set of axioms like those proposed by Fairservis for the Indus Valley were valid, they could have very important application all over the world. Furthermore, because of Fairservis's prestige, I anticipate that other archaeologists may well attempt to apply them. However, they are so vague as to their form, and so unproven as to their validity, that they should not be allowed to go unchallenged. I wish to discuss each of Fairservis's axioms in turn, pointing out both the ways in which they are too vague to be applied easily, and the ways in which they may be contradicted by evidence.

Axiom 1 begins: 'Sharply differing cultural assemblages, but contemporary, with significant time depth demonstrated in the local stratigraphy, represent differences of language, whether or not from the same family.'

The very words in which the axiom is stated raise problems: even if we assume agreement as to what is allowed to constitute a 'cultural assemblage', there will inevitably be room for diverse opinions as to how great a difference must exist in order for things to be called 'sharply differing', or about how great a time depth is to be regarded as 'significant'. However, giving a middle-of-the-road interpretation to these terms, it seems to me that the axiom does not fit well with the facts of several present-day cultures. For instance, in modern Maharashtra, or in a European country like Spain, 'cultural assemblages' from an urban center like Bombay or Madrid, as compared with those from a peasant village, could well be seen as 'sharply differing', even though contemporary, and even though both would show continuity over 'significant time depth'; yet they would both correspond to the Marathi or the Spanish language respectively—or, at most, to different dialects of those languages. Fairservis's Axiom 1 continues:

'If the assemblages are far apart geographically, this can mean fundamental differences in language going so far as to the basic stock.'

Now we encounter another difficulty in Fairservis's wording: 'This can mean fundamental differences'. The word 'can' suggests that the implication either may or may not be valid. I assume that Fairservis believes that it is valid most of the time. But here we may continue our consideration of Spanish language and culture: what if one compares Madrid to a peasant village in, say, Uruguay? (I choose a Latin American country in which the American Indian cultures were extinguished immediately after the Conquest, so that there is no continuity between indigenous and European traditions.) If four hundred years can be considered 'significant time depth', then this will be a further counter-example to Fairservis's statement, since both assemblages will, again, correspond to the Spanish language.

Here of course I am comparing 'cultural assemblages' in which at least one is from an industrial society. It is possible that Fairservis means his axioms to apply only to pre-industrial society; however, he states no such qualification. We must ask a serious question, to which no answer may be yet available: are correlations between culture and language, whatever they may be, different in industrial societies than they are in pre-industrial ones?

Axiom 2 is: 'Sharply differing cultural assemblages without significant time depth demonstrated by local stratigraphies represent different languages but not necessarily different language families.'

Here a possible counter-example might be provided by comparing an industrial community with an agricultural community, each founded within the last hundred years in adjacent areas of the United States and of Mexico. In the United States, even the agricultural communities would show relatively great mechanization, and thus could probably not be considered as 'sharply differing'. In Mexico, by contrast, many agricultural communities remain relatively unmechanized, by comparison to the industrial cities. But the two types of Mexican community both use Spanish, just as the two communities in the U.S. both use English. The Mexican case thus seems to falsify Fairservis's Axiom 2.

Axiom 3 is as follows: 'Moderately differing cultural assemblages which, however, share core traits, may represent dialectal differences of the same language.'

Again we have difficulties with Fairservis's wording: first we have to decide what are to be regarded as 'core traits', and then we have to deal with the expression 'may represent dialectal differences'. The use of the word 'may' seems to imply an equal and opposite 'may not', in which case the 'axiom' makes no claim at all. In fact, the only real meaning that can be attached to the 'axiom' is that, when moderately differing cultural assemblages share core traits, they USUALLY or NORMALLY represent dialectal differences of the same languages. But such a claim can be tested by imagining an archaeologist of the year 5000 AD, comparing the remains of 20th century New York, Bombay, and Tokyo. He might conclude that the cultural assemblages from those cities, while 'moderately differing', nevertheless shared 'core traits', namely those of Western European civilization; but he would be wildly incorrect in concluding that the inhabitants spoke dialects of a single language. If one does not wish to consider industrial civilizations, one can look to ancient Mesopotamia, in which the Akkadians and the Sumerians had virtually the same material culture, although their languages were of completely different stocks: Akkadian was a Semitic language, but the genetic connections of Sumerian are much more obscure.

Fairservis's Axiom 4 is: 'Sharply differing cultural assemblages which share trade goods can represent different languages, but can be presumed to have developed a lingua franca.'

Here, if we manage to surmount the ambiguity of the word 'can', we may consider another modern example: Trade goods from Japan, such as transistor radios, are now found all over the world; but certainly no single 'lingua franca' covers the same area.

Axiom no. 5 is as follows: 'Stratigraphical representation of the imposition of a new cultural assemblage upon an older one, but which does share a considerable number of traits in common (some of which must be core) demonstrates linguistic integration of some form: for example, the rule of the Indo-European speaking Hyksos elite over the non-Indo-European speaking Egyptians in the Second Intermediate period, or the creation of a pidgin such as Anglo-Indian.'

This seems to say that a mixture of cultural elements indicates some kind of linguistic 'integration'. A possible counter-example is provided by the Navajo, an American Indian tribe of the Southwestern United States, who have adopted many items of European material culture, but are famous for their resistance to linguistic borrowing.

Thus, although the automobile has been thoroughly integrated into present-day Navajo culture, the terminology relating to automobiles is provided entirely by new coinages within the Navajo language, not by borrowing from English.

As regards Fairservis's 'Anglo-Indian' example, I assume he refers to the variety of English spoken by educated people in India. It is of course true that Indian English shows characteristics derived from the phonology, grammar, and semantics of the Dravidian and Indo-Aryan languages. But linguists use the word 'pidgin' to refer to trade-languages, of markedly hybrid origin and of greatly simplified grammar; I doubt if any linguist would apply the term 'pidgin' to Indian English. It thus remains unclear what kind of degree of linguistic interaction or 'integration' Fairservis has in mind in his Axiom no. 5.

Finally, Axiom no. 6 is: 'Cultural assemblage conformity from site to site demonstrates language conformity.'

A modern counter-example might be provided by 'cultural assemblages' from opposite sides of certain international borders, e.g., that between France and Germany: one would find little in material culture to correspond to the difference in language. Similarly in India, one might look on opposite sides of the border between Andhra and Orissa; again, the differences in material culture would be minor in comparison to the difference between the Dravidian and the Indo-Aryan language structures. Looking to non-industrial cultures, we have many American Indian examples: thus, in northwestern California, the Yurok, Karok, and Hupa tribes have been famous, since the time of Edward Sapir, for sharing a single culture, while nevertheless speaking languages of three completely separate stocks.

Since Fairservis's axioms contain so many vaguely defined terms, as well as 'may's' and 'can's', we might assume he intends them as statements of tendencies, rather than as absolute laws. But then, unless some statistical measures of probability are attached to them, it is not clear to me what their value is. My conclusion is not that Fairservis's account of Indus Valley prehistory is necessarily wrong, but rather that it must share the weakness of his axioms. Like many other archaeologists, Fairservis is all too ready to draw linguistic conclusions from archaeological data; and his reputation is such that other archaeologists and historians may well accept his proposals uncritically. Linguists must therefore continue to repeat that the study of potsherds can never, in itself, reveal anything about language. Fortunately, the continuing analysis of linguistic data is constantly adding to our knowledge of prehistoric Dravidian language and culture; I refer in particular to the work of Franklin Southworth (1975, 1978), and to David McAlpin's evidence for linguistic relationship between Dravidian and Elamite (1974, 1975). Our hypotheses of linguistic history must not fly in the face of non-linguistic data, but they cannot be DETERMINED by archaeological considerations.

11

Written and Spoken Language in South Asia

In 1964 I had the pleasure of organizing a conference on sociolinguistics at UCLA, the proceedings of which were subsequently published (Bright 1966). For me, and for other participants in the conference who had worked in India, such as John Gumperz and Paul Friedrich, the field of sociolinguistics had taken shape as a very direct result of our experiences in South Asia. We had gone there with backgrounds in post-Bloomfieldian structural linguistics, but we had returned with the realization that new methodologies were needed to cope with such phenomena as diglossia, code-switching, widespread multilingualism, and social dialect. (For a survey of the whole literature which has grown up on these topics in South Asia, see Shapiro and Schiffman 1981.)

Among the phenomena with which we were poorly prepared to deal was the relationship between written and spoken language in South Asia, which has several aspects. One is the multiplicity of writing systems, and the fact that radically different scripts are sometimes used for very similar speech varieties, as in the case of Hindi and Urdu. Another aspect was the diglossic distinction between 'literary' and 'colloquial' language—complicated by the fact that 'literary' language is not simply the written variety, but more accurately that of formal speech. Still another aspect involved some paradoxical attitudes towards written language: on the one hand, high prestige is attached to literacy, but on the other hand, where the most prestigious literary texts of all are involved—the Vedas, and later Sanskrit literature as well—great value is set upon oral transmission and memorization. But in considering the complexity of written language in India, we were at a disadvantage in the 1950s, since few of us were experienced in studying written language as such: the post-Bloomfieldian dogma was that writing was in fact only a secondary reflection of REAL language.

It is in fact only in the last few years that many general linguists have begun to take written language seriously. (Let me refer to just one field which currently seems to be coming into its own with the help of sociolinguistic insights: this is the study of the social functions of written language and of literacy, as related to and compared with the functions of spoken language—cf. Goody 1977, Tannen 1982a, b). The American 'structuralist' linguists of the 1930s through the 1970s were frequently involved in research on previously unwritten American Indian languages; perhaps in reaction to the 'philological' outlooks of their predecessors, they tended to emphasize speech, and to see writing as a mere derivative—not truly worthy of being called 'language'. By contrast, the school of transformational generative grammarians, who came into prominence from the 1960s onward, were concerned at first mainly with English and other standardized languages; and perhaps in counter-reaction to the structuralists' views, they went in a different direction as regards speech vs. writing. On the one hand, since generative syntax dealt most often with major world languages, presented in standard orthography, it was taken for granted that writing was indeed a form of language; but relationships or differences between what is written and what is spoken were generally ignored. On the other hand, generative phonology, as codified in Chomsky and Halle's *Sound Pattern of English* (1968), offered the startling proposal that English orthography—previously maligned by linguists as seriously out of correspondence with the modern spoken language—could in fact be seen as very close to a psychologically real 'underlying representation' of English pronunciation; but again, the generativists tended to ignore the characteristics which DIFFERENTIATE the basic structure of written language from that of speech. Recently, however, a more balanced view, informed by sociolinguistic awareness, seems to be gaining prominence. Many researchers would now say that language has at least three MANIFESTATIONS: spoken, written, and signed (as in the sign language used by the deaf). Written language, especially in societies with long traditions of literacy and of highly valued written literature, tends to acquire its own distinctive structures on all levels: phonology, grammar, semantics, and discourse—and its own sociolinguistic functions in terms of class dialect, register, etc. It is within this framework that I wish to examine the history of spoken and written language in South Asia.[1]

1. Historical Origins of Writing in South Asia

One of the world's significant early scripts is, of course, that of the Indus Valley civilization, often called Harappan, after one of the main archaeological sites. The known inscriptions in this writing system, which has not yet been deciphered, date from around the first half of the third millennium BC, at a period when most scholars believe that Sanskrit speakers had not yet entered the Indus Valley. It is widely hypothesized that the language of the Harappan civilization belonged to the Dravidian family, for two reasons. First, although languages of that group are now concentrated in South India, they are known to have occupied a wider area in the past; and one Dravidian language, Brahui, is still spoken in Baluchistan, just west of the Indus Valley. Second, a significant number of Dravidian borrowings can be identified in the oldest Vedic texts, reflecting the earliest period of contact between Sanskrit speakers and the ancient Harappan population (Emeneau 1954). However, the corpus of Harappan writing is limited primarily to very short texts—typically of five or six characters—found almost exclusively on about 2,500 stone seals, and in clay impressions of those seals. Since some of the impressions are found still attached to bales of trade goods, it is inferred that a major function of the writing was in labeling merchandise. But no bilingual inscriptions have been found; and although two large (and overlapping) concordances of the Harappan inscriptions have been published (Mahadevan 1977, Koskenniemi et al. 1973), all attempts at decipherment still remain speculative—though there are indications that the script was basically logographic, with some development in the direction of phonologically defined signs.[2]

One of the most surprising things about the Harappan script is that it seems to have disappeared from use along with the decline of the

Indus Valley civilization—leaving South Asia with no trace of a writing system for some 2,000 years, until, in the third century BC, two scripts, Brāhmī and Kharoṣṭhī, made their appearance in the stone-carved edicts by which the Emperor Aśoka Maurya propagated Buddhist principles throughout the subcontinent. I deliberately say 'no trace of a writing system', because various scholars have found it hard to believe that anything so valuable as a writing system could be simply discarded, and have looked for evidence that the Harappan script may have simply gone 'underground'. On the one hand, they have pointed to the so-called 'graffiti' which are found on potsherds from all over South Asia during the post-Harappan period, and some of which bear geometrical resemblances to Harappan characters. But since these graffiti lack the patterned nature characteristic of writing systems, and since there is in any case no way to match them phonologically or semantically with Harappan characters, most scholars have regarded them as mere potters' marks (Gupta and Ramachandran 1979:xxi). On the other hand, some writers have called attention to graphic similarity between Harappan signs and those used in the later Brāhmī script; but again, in the absence of phonetic correspondences, these similarities cannot be taken seriously as anything but accidental coincidences of universal geometrical patterns. Another argument is that writing must have existed continuously in South Asia, but that it was on perishable materials, such as cloth or bark, which have not survived (cf. Pandey 1957:16). On this hypothesis, the Aśokan texts are significant for the history of writing only because they were the first of their type to be carved in stone, and therefore to endure. But the Harappans had inscribed their characters not only in stone and clay, but also in other durable materials, such as ivory and copper; so it is difficult to believe that the extensive archaeological research which has been carried out in South Asia would not have turned up SOME examples of pre-Aśokan writing, if any such had indeed existed. Some fragmentary pre-Aśokan inscriptions on coins, plaques, vases etc. have indeed have reported; but all of these turn out to be vulnerable to skepticism as regards date (cf. Goyal 1979:30–45).

Such considerations have led scholars such as Goyal (1979), Verma (1971, 1979), Dani (1963), and Upasak (1960) to claim that pre-Mauryan India was essentially scriptless, and even that the Kharoṣṭhī and Brāhmī scripts were developed under direct orders from the Emperor Aśoka himself. To the latter hypothesis, Gupta and Ramachandran (1979:

123–24) object that 'We do not have a single reference from the ancient world regarding a king or emperor inventing a totally new script and popularizing it'—but of course the Korean King Sejong (1419–52) is traditionally said to have done precisely that (Jensen 1969:211).

2. The Aśokan Scripts

The edicts of the Emperor Aśoka, dating from around 253–250 BC, are found over a large part of South Asia, and in several writing systems. On the northwestern frontier, some inscriptions are in Greek and Aramaic—the principal languages of foreign contact in that area. Most other inscriptions are in the Prakrit dialect of Aśoka's capital in Magadha (now part of Bihar state, in eastern India); but they are in two different writing systems. One of these, Kharoṣṭhī, was written from right to left, like Aramaic and other Semitic scripts; it was used only in the northwest, and eventually died out. The other script, Brāhmī, was written mainly from left to right; it was used in the larger part of the subcontinent, and eventually developed into the many different major and minor scripts used down to the present time in India and Southeast Asia. Both systems were phonologically based, and they introduced a novel method of transcribing both consonants and vowels in a systematic way. Instead of writing both consonantal and vocalic phonemes as independent letters, as is done in Greek, or writing the vowels only as inconsistent or optional diacritics to consonant symbols, as is done in many Semitic writing systems (e.g. Hebrew, Aramaic, and Arabic), the new Indic scripts adopted the strategy of writing each CV sequence as a unit (called in Sanskrit an *akṣara*), specifically by regarding the short vowel *a* as inherent in all consonant symbols, and by writing all other vowels as OBLIGATORY diacritics—attached to the top, to the bottom, or to either side of the consonant. Table 11.1 illustrates the system for Kharoṣṭhī, Brāhmī, and two important major scripts of the present day—(Deva)Nāgarī, used for Hindi and other north Indian languages, and the Kannada script of South India. Compare the rightmost column, which shows how the same syllable would be written in the Urdu adaptation of the Arabic script; note that here the superior line which marks *a,* the inferior line which marks *i,* and the superior curl which marks *u* and *o* are all optional, used mainly in students' primers.[3]

TABLE 11.1. Indic and Semitic Consonant Symbols.

	Kharoṣṭhi	Brahmi	Nȧgari	Kannaḍa	(Urdu)
ka	𐨐	𑀓	क	ಕ	کَ
kȧ		𑀓𑀸	का	ಕಾ	کَا
kı	𐨐𐨁	𑀓𑀺	कि	ಕಿ	کِ
ki		𑀓𑀻	की	ಕೀ	کِی
ku	𐨐𐨂	𑀓𑀼	कु	ಕು	کُ
ku̇		𑀓𑀽	कू	ಕೂ	کُو
ke	𐨐𐨅	𑀓𑁂	के	ಕೆ	کے
kė				ಕೇ	
ko	𐨐𐨆	𑀓𑁄	को	ಕೊ	کو
kȯ				ಕೋ	

It is of interest to note that there is perhaps only one other writing system in the world which indicates CV combinations by vowel diacritics obligatorily attached to consonants. This is the Ethiopic, which is well known to have been derived from South Semitic sources around AD 350 (cf. Jensen 1969:343–44). Writing systems such as these have created problems for scholars who have attempted typologies of writing systems. A system which writes consonants and vowels separately and independently, as in most European languages, is called an alphabet; a system with a unitary symbol for each CV combination, like Japanese *kana* or Sequoyah's Cherokee script, is called a syllabary. But we lack a name to distinguish a system like the Semitic, where a single symbol can indicate *k, ka, ki, ku* etc. And we also need a separate term for the systems used in South Asia and in Ethiopia, which differentiate *ka, ki,* and *ku* by single yet complex symbols, in which consonantal and vocalic elements are combined (cf. Voegelin and

Voegelin 1961). The term 'semi-syllabary' has been suggested, and may prove useful.

These questions are of more than merely terminological importance, as is illustrated in the influential textbook on writing by Gelb (cf. Verma 1971:2–4). On the other hand, Gelb wishes to establish a general principle that 'writing . . . must pass through the stages of logography, syllabography, and alphabetography in this, and no other order'; hence, he says, 'it is absurd to speak of the development of the Ethiopic (or Sanskrit) syllabaries from a Semitic alphabet'. Rather, he wants to say that 'both the Ethiopic and Sanskrit writings are further developments from a Semitic syllabary' (Gelb 1963:201). Elsewhere, however, Gelb declares that Brāhmī letter forms were 'freely invented' (144). And in still another passage (188), Gelb admits that the terms 'alphabet' and 'syllabary' are inadequate, not only for Indic and Ethiopic scripts, but for those of the modern Semitic languages as well. It appears that a universal evolutionary progression, such as Gelb proposes, will need to be based on a more adequate typology of script types.

As has been noted, some writers have proposed that both Kharoṣṭhī and Brāhmī scripts were new inventions within South Asia, in spite of the fact that we have no evidence concerning the process of their development. Other writers have accepted the likelihood that Kharoṣṭhī was an adaptation from the Aramaic script, considering the facts that they were used in the same northwestern area, that they were both written from right to left, and that a fair number of Kharoṣṭhī symbols show significant similarities in shape and pronunciation to the corresponding Aramaic symbols. However, some of these writers have denied that Brāhmī can have the same Aramaic inspiration; they point to the fact that Brāhmī was written in the opposite direction, and that it is harder to find significant correspondences in shape and sound. In this view, Brāhmī must represent either a survival of the Harappan writing system, or an independent new invention. Finally, still other writers, including most European Indologists (especially Bühler), have believed that Brāhmī WAS derived from Aramaic writing; they mention that a few Brāhmī inscriptions are written from right to left, or else partially in the boustrophedon style of alternating directions, and they point to the undoubted similarities of certain Brāhmī letters to those of similar sound in Aramaic, e.g. *g*. All scholars, to be sure, recognize the important fact that both Kharoṣṭhī and Brāhmī scripts were systematically expanded, with reference to any known previous model, so as to convey all the phonological contrasts in place of articulation and manner of articulation which are characteristic of Sanskrit, Prakrit, and of South Indian languages generally; it is clear that the Kharoṣṭhī and Brāhmī scripts as we know them were elaborated by ancient pandits who had a high degree of sophistication in phonetics. (For tables showing the symbols of the relevant Semitic and Indic scripts, see Jensen 1969:302, 316, 365, 367.)

I believe that scholars have not given enough attention to one particular argument in favor of a Semitic origin for the Aśokan scripts. This is their unusual character, described above, whereby vowels are indicated as obligatory diacritics attached to consonant symbols. The only other writing system known to use this principle is the Ethiopic, which is clearly derived from Semitic sources. It seems to me that the Ethiopic and the Indic developments can be accounted for in the same way, as an extension of the Semitic practice of writing vowels as OPTIONAL diacritics; thus even if one is disinclined to see the letter shapes of Kharoṣṭhī and Brāhmī as derived from Semitic sources, it is nevertheless likely that the Indic PRINCIPLE of vowel-writing can be explained as an instance of 'stimulus diffusion' from a Semitic model. However, another problem is even more difficult: was Brāhmī script, or some predecessor of it, used during the 2,000 years that preceded Aśoka's reign? Or was Sanskrit literature, from the Vedic through the Classic periods, composed and transmitted in a purely oral medium? This has been a matter of intense controversy.

3. Orality vs. Literacy in Ancient India

The majority view among European Indologists has been that Sanskrit-speaking culture was basically oral; that not only the Vedas, but also the Brāhmaṇas, the Purāṇas, the epics, and Classic literature in general were composed and transmitted orally; and that even that epitome of sophistication, the Sanskrit grammar of Pāṇini, was elaborated without the use of writing. But other scholars, especially in India, have insisted that a continuous tradition of literacy must have existed, though the written documents themselves have not survived. The problem is that, even though we find mention of writing in Classical Sanskrit texts, it is hard to determine the exact period from which a text dates, and even harder to rule out the possibility that the references to writing are late interpolations. I will attempt to summarize the major types of evidence which bear on this dispute.

3.1. THE GREEK EVIDENCE. The most easily datable evidence is that from the Greek writers who visited India during and following the time of Alexander the Great (cf. Gopal 1977). This material is in some ways unsatisfactory, since it consists largely of fragments quoted by later Greek and Roman authors; furthermore, there is a tendency in much Greek writing on India to emphasize the spectacular and fabulous. However, a few statements seem straightforward and relevant. First, Nearchos, a general of Alexander's army, was reported by Strabo's *Geography* as stating that 'the Hindus wrote letters *(epistolás)* on linen cloth that is very closely woven' (Jones 1930:7.117). However, in an adjacent passage, Strabo also quotes Nearchos as saying, of the ancient Indians, that 'their laws, some public and some private, are unwritten'. It has been supposed that, in speaking of 'laws', Nearchos was referring to *smṛti,* the Sanskrit term literally meaning 'remembered', which is applied to post-Vedic literature known to have been transmitted orally from early times. A possible interpretation for the evidence from Nearchos, then, is that writing was known, and perhaps used for commercial purposes, but not for religious or legal texts.

Second, the Roman writer Quintus Curtius, in his *History of Alexander the Great,* cities an unknown Greek source as stating that 'the tender side of the bark of trees receives written characters like paper'; the reference is evidently to birch bark. These two quotations indicate that writing was known at least in some parts of South Asia around 326 BC.

On the other side of the balance, however, is a much-quoted statement by the Greek envoy Megasthenes, who some 25 years later visited the emperor Candragupta Maurya, known to the Greeks as Sandracottus. Megasthenes commented on the lack of serious crime in ancient India, and his observations were recorded by Strabo as follows (in the translation of Jones 1930:7.86–89): 'Megasthenes says that when he was in the camp of Sandracottus, although the number in camp was forty thousand, he on no day saw reports of stolen articles that were worth more than 200 drachmae; and that too among a people who use unwritten laws only. For, he continues, they have no knowledge of written letters, and regulate every single thing from memory. . . .'

This quotation has been cited by many scholars to indicate that, at least in the parts of South Asia visited by Megasthenes, oral transmission was still dominant. However, some of the terminology in the quotation is troubling: if Megasthenes 'on no day saw reports of stolen articles' worth over 200 drachmae, this clearly implies WRITTEN reports. However, examination of the original Greek text suggests a more appropriate translation: *mēdemían heméran ideīn anēnegména klémmata* is literally 'not-one day to-see brought-back stolen-articles'. That is, the participle *anēnegména,* which Jones translated as 'reported', could equally well refer to stolen articles RECOVERED. This fits better with the statement by Megasthenes that no writing system was in use during the reign of Candragupta Maurya—only about 50 years before the time of the Aśokan inscriptions.

It has been suggested that Megasthenes, like Nearchos before him, observed that justice was regulated by the oral *smṛti* tradition, and that he then jumped to a false conclusion that writing was not used at all (cf. Gopal 1977:51). At any rate, the Greek evidence as a whole can be interpreted in terms of the hypotheses already stated: that, in the early Mauryan period, writing existed in some parts of South Asia, perhaps used for certain limited purposes, but not used for law or administration. (It should be noted, however, that Gopal 1977, after carefully marshalling his evidence, wishes to use it to argue for the creation of the Brāhmī script in the early Mauryan period: I cannot agree that such a conclusion is required.)

3.2. THE BUDDHIST TRADITION. Since the Brāhmī texts are in fact the Buddhist edicts of the Emperor Aśoka, it is natural to look to other early Buddhist texts for evidence of writing. Such evidence is found in the Pali scriptures, as reported by Rhys Davids (1903:107–20). The oldest reference is in the *Sīlas,* thought to date from around 400 BC, which contains a list of frivolous activities forbidden to Buddhist monks; one is called *akkharika,* i.e. the tracing of *akṣaras* or written symbols on the skin of a person who is then supposed to guess what is written. In the *vinaya* texts of perhaps a century later, the term *lekha* 'writing' first occurs, as the name of a skill which monks were allowed to learn, and which was used both for official notices and for personal letters. However, as Rhys Davids notes (1903:109), 'it is a long step from the use of writing for such notifications . . . to the use

. . . for the purpose of writing down any books'. And in fact the Pali literature strongly suggests the absence of anything that could be called 'scriptures'. For one thing, the monastic rules give detailed lists of all objects which monks were allowed to own, or not allowed; but there is no reference to books or manuscripts. Again, the *Anguttara Nikāya* refers to the danger that religious texts will be lost if the chain of oral transmission is broken; and a definition of scholarship is given which does not mention reading, but rather 'repeating over to oneself'. If, in a monastic settlement, no member knows the 227 Rules of the Order, it is prescribed that a monk shall be sent to a neighboring group to learn the material by heart; this is to be done even if it violates a rule forbidding monks to travel during the rainy season.

It should be noted that it is difficult to assign dates to the early Buddhist texts, or to rule out the possibility of subsequent changes or additions. However, Buddhist tradition ascribes the oral formulation of the Pali canon to the first century after the Buddha's death, and it was supposedly not written down until the first century BC. Whatever the accuracy of these dates, they strongly point toward the same hypothesis suggested by the Greek data—namely that, in the early Mauryan period, writing was used in India for certain purposes, but that oral transmission was obligatory, to the exclusion of writing, for the extensive and important texts of the sacred Buddhist canon.

3.3. THE HINDU TRADITION. It is well known that oral transmission of the Vedas and other Sanskrit literature has been practiced in India from ancient times to the present. In fact, the earliest record of written Sanskrit dates from only the first century BC (Verma 1979:106)—much later than the Prakrit inscriptions, at a time when Sanskrit can no longer have been widely spoken. Yet some earlier writings in Sanskrit must have been on perishable material, and so vanished. Scholars differ as to their estimates of the dates when writing is first referred to in Sanskrit literature, and when it was first USED for literary purposes. However, the general view of European scholars in the twentieth century is typified by the following quotations:

> References to writing occur . . . in the Sūtra literature [sixth to second centuries BC], but there is no clear mention of it in the Vedas, Brāh-

> maṇas or Upaniṣads. This negative evidence, however, is not wholly conclusive, and some form of script may have been used by merchants. . . . (Basham 1954:394)

> During the period when the Vedic civilisation was being built up, no form of writing was employed in India, and in its absence the technique was evolved of preserving intact the Vedic literature by means of oral tradition. Even when writing was introduced, this oral tradition persisted in the various departments of knowledge, and it continued as a basic feature of Indian education down to modern times . . . use of writing was only slowly adopted in the Brahmin schools, and in the early period its function lay primarily in business and administration. . . . It is unlikely that much literature existed in manuscript form before the second century BC. (Burrow 1955:64–65)

> The first form of the Indian alphabets now used . . . could have been introduced to India about 800 BC . . . and . . . must have been adapted by Sanskrit-speaking, specialists with great finesse, to the Indian phonetic system. . . . The presence of writing is also shown by the terminology of the oldest legal texts, by the canonical literature of the Buddhists and the Jains, by the Rāmāyana, and by reports of the Greeks. [I comment on these points below.] . . . At the beginning, writing served only practical aims. For literary purposes, it entered into usage among the peoples in general only in a secondary and progressive way. But in India, the bearers of literature clung resolutely to the oral tradition for a long time. . . . Dissemination by recitation was frequent, even for secular or semi-secular works, especially the Epic. Brahmanical teaching, including that of grammar, had been entirely oral at a previous date; Pāṇini attests the existence of writing, but not its use in teaching; his grammar, with its supplements, gives reason to believe in a purely oral tradition. (Renou 1957:32–34)[4]

It is necessary to comment on the evidence which Renou mentions regarding writing in Classical Sanskrit times. The Buddhist and Greek materials have been mentioned above. Renou's mention of old legal materials presumably refers to supposed mentions of writing by the Vedic sage Bṛhaspati—but these are, of course, known only through quotations by much later writers. The statesman Kauṭilya composed the *Arthaśāstra,* perhaps the world's first treatise on political science, the received text of which contains many references to writing in an administrative context; but again, we cannot be sure about the date of Kauṭilya himself, or about the antiquity of the received text (cf. Goyal

1979:26–27). Similar qualifications must be applied to mentions of writing in the Jain canon and in the epic.

The testimony related to Pāṇini's Sanskrit grammar, commonly believed to date from the fourth century BC, is discussed further by Agrawala (1963:25):

> The text of the *sūtras* has been handed down to us almost intact by the method of oral transmission by which Sanskrit learning through the ages has descended from generation to generation through a succession of teachers and pupils . . . instead of being conserved in writing. . . .

Memorization is of course aided in this instance by the extreme brevity of Pāṇini's rules; thus his last sutra is *a a*—which, given appropriate 'metarules' of interpretation, is understood as meaning that the phonemic short /a/ is realized as phonetic shwa [ə]. But elsewhere, Agrawala points out (312–13):

> Writing was known in the time of Pāṇini . . . Though teaching was oral in those days, . . . Pāṇini hints at the use of the writing in several significant expressions. These are (1) *grantha* ['book'], (2) *lipikara,* a writer, [and] *yavanāni lipi* ['Greek writing']. . . .

It is significant to recall that Pāṇini lived in the northwest, where he was most likely to be aware of Greek, Aramaic, or Persian scripts; and indeed, his term *lipi* 'writing' is apparently a loanword into Sanskrit from Old Persian *dipi.*

The evidence of the Pāṇinian tradition and of other early materials thus all point toward the likelihood that writing was known and used in South Asia from a date in pre-Mauryan times which we cannot specify exactly, but that it was probably restricted mainly to commercial and other practical purposes, and only adapted to sacred or secular literature in later times. This in turn suggests that the tradition of oral composition and of verbatim transmission was maintained in India well into the Classic period of Sanskrit literature.

In opposition to the above views, however, some Indian scholars—perhaps from patriotic motives—have not only denied that the Aśokan scripts could have been derived from a foreign source, but have also maintained that writing has existed in India since Vedic times.[5] Thus Wakankar (1983, unpaginated) writes:

> According to Indian tradition it is [the god] Ganesha, the younger son of Shiva Maheshwara, who created the . . . logical Phono-graphy [and] incised the Letters after the Mantras delivered by Shiva. . . . To state that all these [Vedic hymns, in diverse meters] were composed without aid of writing and without aid of counting each letter is unbelievable . . . Shiva Maheshwara is the most popular deity of South India; but in the grammatic tradition he is the earliest of the Grammarians . . . the first grammarian is identified with Nataraja Shiva; the Sound categories are attributed to Shiva who is fond of going into cosmic dance. . . . [T]he sages . . . went to him for acquiring some device to save the Vedas from being lost. Understanding their worries, Nataraja Shiva Maheshwara gave them 14 aphorisms, called Shivasootras, delivering them by striking his trinklet.

[The Sívasūtras are a listing of the morphophonemic classes into which Pāṇini divides the Sanskrit phonemes; they are traditionally given as a sort of prologue to his grammar. The term 'trinklet' is Wakankar's rather strange translation of Sanskrit *ḍamāru*, a type of hand drum.]

> Shiva Maheshwara's Categories of Sound trickled down to the Grammarian Panini. . . . Now we come to Ganesha, the First of the School of Vedic scribes. . . . *Ganesha-Keelaka* says in clear terms that He (Ganesha) incised writing . . . inspired by the Mantras of Shiva enunciated earlier. . . .

I will not attempt to comment in detail on Wakankar's mythological account of the origin of Sanskrit speech and of writing; however, it is striking that he believes the Vedas and their meters COULD not have been elaborated without the use of writing. Yet the metrical structures of the Vedas, like the melodic patterns traditionally associated with the various meters of Classical Sanskrit poetry, can never have been a complication, but rather an aid to the memory; we can always remember the words to a song better than we can those of purely spoken poetry, and those of poetry better than prose. Furthermore, it seems to me a tribute to Hindu culture, rather than an act of derogation, to recognize that a complex literature could be developed and perpetuated by the human mind and memory alone, without the 'artificial' extension of writing systems.

4. Other Parts of the World

The roles of literacy and orality in South Asia may profitably be compared with what is known from other regions where oral traditions have been important. The famous studies by Lord (1960) and Parry (1971) on the oral epic in southeastern Europe show that oral narratives still chanted by peasant bards in Yugoslavia are based not on verbatim repetition, but on a constant overall pattern within which individual performers can use varying recombinations of formulaic expressions—and also show that a similar process is likely to have given rise to the Homeric epics of preliterate Ancient Greece. Goody (1977:116–20) reports the same processes in present-day oral literatures of West Africa; so it may well be that Classical Sanskrit literature—and even the Vedas—originated in such structures of 'controlled improvisation'. But India, from a very ancient date, perfected the skills of word-for-word repetition and memorization, and institutionalized them for Hindu, Buddhist, and secular literature. Parallels, with less historical depth, can be found elsewhere in the world. Finnegan (1973, 1977) reports extensive verbatim memorization in West Africa (in cultures different from those studied by Goody), and so does Sherzer (1982:319–20, n. 2) for the Cuna Indians of Panama. Field workers among North American Indian groups, such as myself among the Karok of northwestern California, have heard how, less than 100 years ago, children were required to repeat each sentence of the myths narrated by their grandparents, so as to ensure accurate transmission. Where musical features of rhythm and melody are involved, the human memory can of course stretch even farther; consider a singer in our own society who has memorized words and music for twenty or thirty full-length operas—or the symphony conductor who works without a score. Again in our own society, we can consider the extensive repertories of numerous musicians, in the folk and jazz traditions, who cannot read a note of written music.

Thus there is reason to believe that the capacities of human memory, though they may have been neglected and downgraded by modern European societies, are in fact—with proper training—capable of the prodigies of retention which have long been customary in Hindu culture. Doubts concerning such capacities, such as those quoted above from Wakankar, are to be sure also expressed by some Western writers, as in the extensive work on literacy and orality by Ong (e.g.

1982:65–67)—though he concedes the Cuna evidence presented by Sherzer. My own belief is that there is no serious reason to deny that the human mind can perform awesome feats of memory, in situations where a culture has developed a tradition for such practice, and where major prestige is attached to oral transmission. This is where we must think sociolinguistically, in terms of ATTITUDES toward speech vs. writing as alternative manifestations of language.

5. Conclusion

A traditional Indian view is expressed by Ananda Coomaraswamy as follows (1947:27):

> From the Indian point of view a man can only be said to KNOW what he knows by HEART; what he must go to a book to be reminded of, he merely knows of. . . . From the earliest times, Indians have thought of the learned man, not as one who has read much, but as one who has been profoundly taught.

It appears, then, that a society may have knowledge of writing, and yet assign it to restricted functions—the use of merchants, perhaps, as opposed to the purposes of religion or of literary art. A possible parallel comes from Minoan Greece: the Mycenaean civilization used the Linear A and B scripts for bills of lading, cargo manifests, etc.: but so far as we know, they did not use them for literature. Following the collapse of Minoan civilization, Greece apparently did without a writing system for some centuries, until the Phoenician-based alphabet was introduced; during this period, of course, the *Iliad* and the *Odyssey* were in the oral tradition, taking the forms which we now know—just as in India, around the same time, the Hindus were apparently also producing and transmitting literature without the aid of writing.

A parallel from a different branch of culture comes from Native America. It is generally said that the American Indian did not use the wheel. This is true, except that the Aztecs (and their Meso-American neighbors) DID know about wheels—but they used them only on children's toys. It was not that these people lacked the ability to invent the wheel, but rather that they chose not to ascribe any important function to it (Vaillant 1950:153).

It is useful to remember that Plato, who lived when the alphabet was a relative novelty in Greece, warned that it would corrupt human memories, fostering both credulity and mistrust (Jowett 1892:1.484–88). For centuries afterwards, Latin and Greek were normally read ALOUD, the written text being conceived basically as an aid to spoken performance; not until AD 384 does St. Augustine report his astonishment on observing that his teacher, St. Ambrose, was capable of reading SILENTLY. In medieval England, written contracts were at first regarded with suspicion: a man's spoken word was his bond, it was felt, but a piece of paper was just a piece of paper (cf. Clanchy 1979). Since then, of course, European society has succumbed to what Jorge Luis Borges (1960) has called 'the cult of the book'; nowadays it is writing, not speech, which most educated people regard as basic, and indeed as a necessity. Nevertheless, to quote Coomaraswamy once more (1947:19), 'necessities are not always goods in themselves, out of their context; some, like wooden legs, are advantageous only to men already maimed'.

NOTES

1. For general references on the history of writing, including South Asian systems, see Gelb (1963), Diringer (1968), and Jensen (1969). For more specific discussions of the history of writing in India, see Bühler (1895, 1896), Pandey (1957), Dani (1963), Sircar (1965), Verma (1971), and Gupta and Ramachandran (1979) (with the review by Salomon 1982).

Versions of this paper have been presented at the University of Washington and the University of Ottawa. I am indebted for encouragement and advice to A. L. Becker, M. V. Deshpande, M. B. Emeneau, Roy Andrew Miller, P. B. Patel, Shana Poplack, Richard Salomon, and Deborah Tannen.

2. For general accounts of this script, and of attempts at its decipherment, see Dani (1963:12–22), Jensen (1969:353–56), Zide and Zvelebil (1970), Bright (1982, 1983). For a recent major effort to decipher the Harappan language in terms of Sanskrit, see Rao (1982).

3. Becker (1984:143–44) has commented that the typical shape of the Indic *akṣara,* as now used even for non-Indic languages such as Burmese, Javanese, and Balinese—consisting of a consonantal center with vocalic marks above, below, before, and after it—has come to be a metaphor in terms of which all other phenomena can be organized. From Zurbuchen (1981:vi) he quotes part of the prologue to a Balinese shadow play, in which the graphemic unit is invoked:

> There is a god unsupported by the divine mother earth,
> Unsheltered by the sky,
> Unilluminated by the sun, moon, stars, or constellations.
> Yes, Lord, you dwell in the void, and are situated thus:
> You reside in a golden jewel,
> Regaled on a golden palanquin,
> Umbrellaed by a floating lotus.
> There approached in audience by all the gods of the cardinal directions . . .

4. For a more recent statement, see Kiparsky (1976:99–103).

5. For a convenient synopsis of such views, see Naik (1971:1.7, 49–51, 77–92, 95–99, 2.611–36).

BIBLIOGRAPHY

Acharya, A. S. 1968. Rabakavi Kannada. *Linguistic Survey Bulletin, Deccan College* 5:14–19.

Acharya, A. S. 1969a. Barkur Kannada. *Linguistic Survey Bulletin, Deccan College* 11:1–8.

Acharya, A. S. 1969b. Tiptur Kannada. *Linguistic Survey Bulletin, Deccan College* 17:17–22.

Agrawala, Vasudeva S. 1963. *India as known to Pāṇini*. 2d ed. Varanasi: Prithvi Kumar.

Ananthanarayana, H. S. 1968. Sound changes in Sanketi, a Tamil dialect. In Krishnamurti 1968, 1–14.

Andronov, Mixail S. 1959. Razgovornye formy tamil'skogo glagola ['Colloquial forms of the Tamil verb']. *Kratkije Soobščenija Instituta Vostokovedenija* (Moscow) 29:16–25.

Arden, Albert H. 1934. *A progressive grammar of common Tamil*. 4th ed. Madras: Christian Literature Society. 5th ed., revised by A. C. Clayton, 1942.

Arden, Albert H. 1937. *A progressive grammar of the Telugu language*. 4th ed. Madras: Christian Literature Society.

Bach, Emmon. 1964. *An introduction to transformational grammars*. New York: Holt, Rinehart & Winston.

Bailey, Sir Harold W. 1975. Indian *Sindhu-*, Iranian *Hindu-*. *Bulletin of the School of Oriental and African Studies, University of London* 38:610–11.

Barth, Ernest A. T. 1961. The language behavior of Negroes and Whites. *Pacific Sociological Review* 4:69–72.

Basham, Arthur L. 1954. *The wonder that was India*. New York: Macmillan.

Becker, Alton L. 1984. Biography of a sentence: A Burmese proverb. In *Text, play, and story: The construction and reconstruction of self and soci-*

ety, ed. Stuart Plattner, 135–55. Washington, D.C.: American Ethnological Society.

Bernstein, Basil. 1964. Elaborated and restricted codes: Their social origins and some consequences. In *The ethnography of communication,* ed. John J. Gumperz and Dell Hymes (*American Anthropologist* 66, no. 6, pt. 2), 55–69. Menasha, Wis.

Biligiri, H. S. 1955. The nasal phonemes of Kannada. *Indian Linguistics* 16:306–8.

Blaylock, Curtis. 1965. Hispanic metaphony. *Romance Philology* 18:253–71.

Bloch, Jules. 1910. Castes et dialectes en tamoul. *Mémoires de la Société de Linguistique de Paris* 16:1–30.

Bloomfield, Leonard. 1933. *Language.* New York: Holt.

Borges, Jorge Luis. 1960. *Otras inquisiciones.* Buenos Aires: Emecé.

Brainerd, B. 1966. Grammars for number names. *Foundations of Language* 1:109–33.

Brandt Corstius, H. 1968. *Grammars for number names.* Dordrecht: Reidel.

Brigel, J. 1872. *A grammar of the Tulu language.* Mangalore: Basel Mission.

Bright, William. 1958a. *An outline of colloquial Kannada.* (Deccan College monograph series no. 22; Indian Linguistics monograph series, no. 1.) Poona: Deccan College and Linguistic Society of India.

Bright, William. 1958b. A note on visarga. *Bulletin of Deccan College* 18:271–73.

Bright, William. 1960a. Linguistic change in some Indian caste dialects. In Ferguson and Gumperz 1960, 19–26. [In this volume, 3–10.]

Bright, William. 1960b. Social dialect and language history. *Current Anthropology* 1:424–25.

Bright, William. 1966a. Dravidian metaphony. *Language* 43:311–22. [In this volume, 19–36.]

Bright, William. 1966b. Language, social stratification, and cognitive orientation. In *Explorations in sociolinguistics,* ed. Stanley Lieberson (*Sociological Inquiry,* 36:2), 313–18. [In this volume, 37–43.]

Bright, William (ed.) 1966c. *Sociolinguistics.* The Hague: Mouton.

Bright, William. 1970. Phonological rules in literary and colloquial Kannada. *Journal of the American Oriental Society* 90:140–44. [In this volume, 65–73.]

Bright, William. 1972a. The enunciative vowel. *International Journal of Dravidian Linguistics* 1:1.26–55. [Revised as Bright 1975.]

Bright, William. 1972b. Hindi numerals. In *Studies in linguistics in honor of George L. Trager,* ed. M. Estellie Smith (Janua linguarum, series maior, no. 52), 222–30. The Hague: Mouton. [In this volume, 74–85.]

Bright, William. 1973. Replies to comments on 'The enunciative vowel'. *International Journal of Dravidian Linguistics* 2:55–63.

Bright, William. 1975. The Dravidian enunciative vowel. In *Dravidian phonological systems,* ed. Harold F. Schiffman and Carol M. Eastman, 11–46. Seattle: South Asian Studies Program, Institute for Comparative and Foreign Area Studies, University of Washington. [In this volume, 86–117.]

Bright, William. 1976. *Variation and change in language*. Stanford, Calif.: Stanford University Press, 1976.

Bright, William. 1982. Review of Mitchiner 1981. *Journal of the American Oriental Society* 102:233–35. [In this volume as 'How not to decipher the Indus Valley inscriptions', 118–23.]

Bright, William. 1984. *American Indian linguistics and literature*. Berlin: Mouton.

Bright, William. 1986. Archaeology, linguistics, and Ancient Dravidian. In *South Asian languages: Structure, convergence and diglossia,* ed. Bh. Krishnamurti, 108–12. Delhi: Motilal Banarsidass. [In this volume, 124–29.]

Bright, William. 1988. Written and spoken language in South Asia. In *On language: Rhetorica, Phonologica, Syntactica. A Festschrift for Robert P. Stockwell,* ed. Caroline Duncan-Rose and Theo Vennemann, 22–38. London: Routledge. [In this volume, 130–47.]

Bright, William, and A. K. Ramanujan. 1962. *A study of Tamil dialects*. Chicago: Committee on South Asian Studies, University of Chicago (mimeographed).

Bright, William, and Marcia Bright. 1976. Archaeology and linguistics in prehistoric Southern California. In Bright 1976, 189–205. Stanford, Calif.: Stanford University Press.

Bright, William, and Jacqueline Lindenfeld. 1968. Complex verb forms in colloquial Tamil. In Krishnamurti 1968, 30–45. [In this volume, 44–64.]

Bright, William, and A. K. Ramanujan. 1964. Sociolinguistic variation and language change. *Proceedings of the Ninth International Congress of Linguists* (Cambridge, Mass.), ed. Horace Lunt, 1107–13. The Hague: Mouton. [In this volume, 11–18.]

Bühler, Georg. 1895. *On the origin of the Indian Brāhma alphabet*. (Indian studies, no. 3.) Wien: Tempsky. Reprinted, Varanasi: Chowkhamba Sanskrit Series, 1963.

Bühler, Georg. 1896. *Indische Palaeographie von circa 350 a.Chr.—circa 1300 p.Chr.* (*Grundriss der indo-arischen Philologie und Altertumskunde* 1:11.) Strassburg: Trübner. Translated as *Indian palaeography* (*Indian Antiquary,* vol. 33, Appendix), 1904. Reprinted, Calcutta: Sambunath Pandit, 1959.

Burrow, Thomas. 1940. Dravidian studies II. *Bulletin of the School of Oriental Studies, University of London* 10:289–97.

Burrow, Thomas. 1946. Dravidian studies V. *Bulletin of the School of Oriental Studies, University of London* 11:595–616.

Burrow, Thomas. 1947. Dravidian studies VI. *Bulletin of the School of Oriental Studies, University of London* 12:132–47.

Burrow, Thomas. 1955. *The Sanskrit language*. London: Faber & Faber.

Burrow, Thomas, and Sudhibhushan Bhattacharya. 1953. *The Parji language*. Hertford: Austin.

Burrow, Thomas, and M. B. Emeneau. 1961. *Dravidian etymological dictionary*. Oxford: Clarendon. 2nd ed., 1984.

Caldwell, Robert. 1913. *A comparative grammar of the Dravidian or South-Indian family of languages*. 3d ed. London: Kegan Paul, Trench, Trubner. Reprinted, Madras: University of Madras, 1956, 1961.

Cardona, George. 1965. *A Gujarati reference grammar*. Philadelphia: University of Pennsylvania Press.

Chatterjee, Suhas. 1962. *A study of the relationship between written and colloquial Bengali*. Dissertation, Hartford Seminary Foundation.

Chatterji, Suniti Kumar. 1926. *The origin and development of the Bengali language*. Vol. 1, *Introduction, Phonology*. Calcutta: University Press. (Reprinted, London: Allen & Unwin; Delhi: Motilal Banarsidass, 1970.)

Chomsky, Noam, and Morris Halle. 1968. *The sound pattern of English*. New York: Harper & Row.

Cingaram, K. 1968. The consonantal system of Tigala, a Tamil dialect. In Krishnamurti 1968, 75–80.

Clanchy, M. T. 1979. *From memory to written record: England, 1066–1307*. London: Arnold. Cambridge, Mass.: Harvard University Press.

Coomaraswamy, Ananda K. 1947. The bugbear of literacy. In *Am I my brother's keeper?*, 19–35. New York: Day.

Dani, Ahmad Hasan. 1963. *Indian palaeography*. Oxford: Clarendon.

Diffloth, Gerard. 1969. The Irula dialect of Tamil. In *Proceedings of the First International Conference-Seminar of Tamil Studies,* ed. Xavier S. Thani Nayagam, 559–62. Kuala Lumpur: International Association of Tamil Research.

Dimock, Edward Cameron, Jr. 1957. Notes on stem-vowel alternation in the Bengali verb. *Indian Linguistics* 17:172–77.

Dimock, Edward Cameron, Jr. 1960. Literary and colloquial Bengali in modern Bengali prose. In Ferguson and Gumperz 1960, 43–58.

Diringer, David. 1968. *The alphabet*. 3d ed. London: Hutchinson.

Ehret, Christopher. 1976. Linguistic evidence and its correlation with archaeology. *World Archaeology,* 8, no. 1:5–18.

Emeneau, Murray B. 1954. Linguistic prehistory of India. *Proceedings of the American Philosophical Society* 98:282–92. [Reprinted in Emeneau 1980, 85–104.]

Emeneau, Murray B. 1956. India as a linguistic area. *Language* 32:3–16. [Reprinted in Emeneau 1980, 105–25.]

Emeneau, Murray B. 1963. Dravidian comparative phonology: A sketch. Berkeley (dittoed). Published, Annamalainagar: Annamalai University, 1970.

Emeneau, Murray B. 1970. Kodagu vowels. *Journal of the American Oriental Society* 90:145–58.

Emeneau, Murray B. 1980. *Language and linguistic area.* Stanford, Calif.: Stanford University Press.

Emeneau, Murray B., and Berend van Nooten. 1968. *Sanskrit sandhi and exercises.* 2d ed. Berkeley: University of California Press.

Fairbanks, Gordon H. 1957. Frequency and phonemics. *Indian Linguistics* 17:105–13.

Fairservis, Walter A., Jr. 1972. The consequences of Harappan as a Dravidian language. Mimeographed. (Paper read at the 76th Annual Meeting, American Anthropological Association, Houston, Texas.)

Fairservis, Walter A., Jr. 1975. *The roots of ancient India.* 2d ed. Chicago: University of Chicago Press.

Ferguson, Charles A. 1959. Diglossia. *Word* 15:325–40.

Ferguson, Charles A., and John J. Gumperz (eds.) 1960. *Linguistic diversity in South Asia.* (Research Center in Anthropology, Folklore, and Linguistics, publication no. 13; *International Journal of American Linguistics,* 26, no. 3, pt. 3.) Bloomington: Indiana University.

Finnegan, Ruth. 1973. Literacy vs. non-literacy: The Great Divide? In *Modes of thought,* ed. Robin Horton and Ruth Finnegan, 112–44. London: Faber & Faber.

Finnegan, Ruth. 1977. *Oral poetry.* Cambridge and New York: Cambridge University Press.

Firth, John R. 1934. Tamil phonetics. Appendix to Arden 1934.

Fischer, John L. 1958. Social influences in the choice of a linguistic variant. *Word* 14:47–56.

Fowler, Murray. 1954. The segmental phonemes of Sanskritized Tamil. *Language* 30:362–67.

Friedrich, Paul. 1961. Review of Ferguson and Gumperz 1960. *Language* 37:163–68.

Gai, Govind Swamirao. 1946. *Historical grammar of Old Kannada.* Poona: Deccan College.

Garvin, Paul L. 1961. Evaluation procedure in linguistic analysis. *Studies in Linguistics* 15:62–69.

Geiger, Wilhelm. 1900. *Litteratur und Sprache der Singhalesen.* Strassburg: Trübner.

Geiger, Wilhelm. 1938. *A grammar of the Sinhalese language.* Colombo: Ceylon Branch, Royal Asiatic Society.

Gelb, Ignace J. 1963. *A study of writing*. 2d ed. Chicago: University of Chicago Press.

Goody, Jack. 1977. *The domestication of the savage mind*. Cambridge and New York: Cambridge University Press.

Gopal, Lallanji. 1977. Early Greek writers on writing in India. In *In commemoration of D. D. Kosambi*, ed. Lallanji Gopal, 41–54. Varanasi: Banaras Hindu University.

Goyal, S. R. 1979. Brahmi—An invention of the Early Mauryan period. In Gupta and Ramachandran 1979, 1–53.

Grignard, A. 1924. *A grammar of the Oraon language*. Calcutta: Catholic Orphan Press.

Gumperz, John J. 1958. Dialect differences and social stratification in a North Indian village. *American Anthropologist* 60:668–82.

Gumperz, John J. and Dell Hymes (eds.) 1964. *The ethnography of communication* (*American Anthropologist*, 66, no. 6, pt. 2.) Menasha, Wis.: American Anthropological Association.

Gupta, S. P., and K. S. Ramachandran (eds.) 1979. *The origin of Brahmi script*. Delhi: D. K. Publications.

Gurreddy, C. Venkata Rama. 1968. The Erukula language. *Linguistic Survey Bulletin, Deccan College* 4:1–6.

Gurubasave Gowda, K. S. 1968. The Sholiga dialect of Kannada. *Linguistic Survey Bulletin, Deccan College* 6:13–18.

Haas, Mary R. 1944. Men's and women's speech in Koasati. *Language* 20:142–49.

Hares, Walter P. 1929. *An English-Punjabi dictionary*. Lahore: Civil & Military Gazette Press.

Harter, Joseph Martin, et al. 1960. *Hindi basic course*. Washington, D.C.: Center for Applied Linguistics.

Hiremath, R. C. 1961. *The structure of Kannada*. Dharwar: Karnatak University.

Hoenigswald, Henry M. 1960. *Language change and linguistic reconstruction*. Chicago: University of Chicago Press.

Hymes, Dell. 1962. The ethnography of speaking. In *Anthropology and human behavior*, ed. Thomas Gladwin and William Sturtevant, 13–53. Washington, D.C: Anthropological Society of Washington.

Hymes, Dell. 1966. Two types of linguistic relativity. In Bright 1966c, 114–58.

Jensen, Hans. 1969. *Sign, symbol, and script*. 3d ed. New York: Putnam.

Jha, Subhadra. 1958. *The formation of the Maithili language*. London: Luzac.

Jones, Horace L. (trans.) 1930. *The Geography of Strabo*. 8 vols. Cambridge, Mass.: Harvard University Press.

Joos, Martin. 1952. The medieval sibilants. *Language* 28:222–31.

Jothimutthu, P. 1956. *A guide to Tamil by the direct method.* Madras: Christian Literature Society.

Jowett, Benjamin (trans.) 1892. *The Dialogues of Plato.* 3d ed. Oxford: Oxford University Press.

Kakati, Banikanta. 1941. *Assamese: Its formation and development.* Gauhati: Department of Historical and Antiquarian Studies.

Kamatchinathan, A. 1969. *The Tirunelvēli Tamil dialect.* (Department of linguistics, publication no. 19.) Annamalainagar: Annamalai University.

Kanapathi Pillai, K. 1935. *A study of the language of the Tamil inscriptions of the 7th and the 8th centuries A.D.* Dissertation, University of London.

Kanapathi Pillai, K. 1943. The enunciative vowel in Dravidian. *University of Ceylon Review* 1:35–41.

Kanapathi Pillai, K. 1958. The Jaffna dialect of Tamil. *Indian Linguistics* 19:219–27.

Kanapathi Pillai, M. 1955. *Practical Tamil.* Paruthithurai, Ceylon.

Karunakaran, K. 1971. *The Kollimalai Tamil dialect.* (Department of Linguistics, publication no. 26.) Annamalainagar: Annamalai University.

Katre, Sumitra Mangesh. 1935. Konkani phonetics. *Journal of the Dept. of Letters, University of Calcutta* 27, no. 4:1–19.

Katwijk, A. van. 1965. A grammar of Dutch number names. *Foundations of Language* 1:51–58.

Kelkar, Ashok R. 1966. A note on Standard Chinese numerals. *Indian Linguistics* 26:196–202.

Kelley, Gerald B. 1959. Telugu vowel phonemes. *Indian Linguistics* 20:146–58.

Kelley, Gerald B. 1963. Vowel phonemes and external vocalic sandhi in Telugu. *Journal of the American Oriental Society* 83:67–73.

Kellogg, Samuel H. 1938. *A grammar of the Hindi language.* 3d ed. London: Routledge & Kegan Paul.

Kinkade, M. Dale, and J. V. Powell. 1976. Language and the prehistory of North America. *World Archaeology* 8, no. 1:83–100.

Kiparsky, Paul. 1976. Oral poetry: Some linguistic and typological considerations. In *Oral literature and the formula,* ed. Benjamin A. Stolz and R. S. Shannon, 73–106. Ann Arbor: Center for the Coordination of Ancient and Modern Studies, University of Michigan.

Kittel, Ferdinand. 1894. *Kannada-English dictionary.* Mangalore: Basel Mission.

Kittel, Ferdinand. 1903. *A grammar of the Kannada language.* Mangalore: Basel Mission.

Knorozov, Yuri V., et al. 1972. *Proto-Indica: 1968.* Moscow: Institute of Ethnography, Academy of Sciences of the USSR.

Koskenniemi, Seppo, et al. 1973. *Materials for the study of the Indus script.* Vol. 1, *A concordance to the Indus inscriptions.* Helsinki: Suomalainen Tiedeakatemia.

Krishnamurti, Bh. 1958a. Alternations *i/e* and *u/o* in South Dravidian. *Language* 34:458–68.

Krishnamurti, Bh. 1958b. Proto-Dravidian **z. Indian Linguistics* 19:259–93.

Krishnamurti, Bh. 1961. *Telugu verbal bases.* (University of California publications in linguistics, no. 24.) Berkeley.

Krishnamurti, Bh. (ed.) 1968. *Studies in Indian linguistics (Prof. M. B. Emeneau Ṣaṣṭipūrti volume).* Poona: Linguistic Society of India.

Kuno, Susumu. 1958. Phonemic structure of colloquial Tamil. *Gengo Kenkyu* (Tokyo) 34:41–62.

Labov, William. 1963. The social motivation of a sound change. *Word* 19:273–309.

Labov, William. 1964. *The social stratification of English in New York City.* Dissertation, Columbia University. Published, Washington, D.C.: Center for Applied Linguistics, 1966.

Lisker, Leigh. 1951. Tamil verb classification. *Journal of the American Oriental Society* 71:111–14.

Lord, Alfred B. 1960. *The singer of tales.* Cambridge, Mass.: Harvard University Press.

McAlpin, David. 1974. Toward Proto-Elamo-Dravidian. *Language* 50:89–101.

McAlpin, David. 1975. Elamite and Dravidian. *Current Anthropology* 16, no. 1:105–15.

McCormack, William. 1960. Social dialects in Dharwar Kannada. In Ferguson and Gumperz 1960, 79–91.

Männer, A. 1886. *Tulu-English dictionary.* Mangalore: Basel Mission. Reprinted, Delhi: Asian Educational Services, 1983.

Mahadevan, Iravatham. 1977. *The Indus script: Texts, concordance and tables.* New Delhi: Archaeological Survey of India.

Mahadevan, Iravatham. 1986. Study of the Indus script: A bilingual approach. In Krishnamurti 1986, 113–19.

Mahadevan, R. 1968a. Kannada dialect of Madurai. *Linguistic Survey Bulletin, Deccan College* 4:13–16.

Mahadevan, R. 1968b. Coimbatore Kannada. *Linguistic Survey Bulletin, Deccan College* 8:15–20.

Manappa Nayak, H. 1967. *Kannada, literary and colloquial: A study of two styles.* Mysore: Rao & Raghavan.

Marr, J. R., and P. Kothandaraman. 1973. Discussion of Bright 1972a. *International Journal of Dravidian Linguistics* 2:47–48.

Matthews, Gordon. 1942. The vulgar pronunciation of Tamil. *Bulletin of the School of Oriental Studies, University of London* 10:992–97.

Mitchiner, John E. 1981. *Studies in the Indus Valley inscriptions*. New Delhi: Oxford & IBH Publ. Co.

Murphy, Raymond J. 1964. Some recent trends in stratification theory and research. *Annals of the American Academy of Political and Social Science* 356:142–67.

Naik, Bapurao S. 1971. *Typography of Devanagari*. 3 vols. Bombay: Directorate of Languages, Government of Maharashtra.

Narasimhia, A. N. 1941. *A grammar of the oldest Kanarese inscriptions*. Mysore: University of Mysore.

Navada, A. V. 1970. Kōta: A Kannada dialect of Mangalore. *Linguistic Survey Bulletin, Deccan College* 20:7–9.

Ong, Walter J., S. J. 1982. *Orality and literacy*. London: Methuen.

Opler, Morris, and Harry Hoijer. 1940. The raid and war-path language of the Chiricahua Apache. *American Anthropologist* 42:617–34.

Pandey, Raj Bali. 1957. *Indian palaeography*. 2d ed. Varanasi: Motilal Banarsidass.

Pandit, Prabodh B. 1955. E and O in Gujrati. *Indian Linguistics* 15:14–54.

Parpola, Asko, et al. 1968. *Decipherment of the Proto-Dravidian inscriptions of the Indus Civilization: A first announcement*. (Scandinavian Institute of Asian Studies, Special publications, no 1.) Copenhagen.

Parpola, Asko, et al. 1969. *Progress in the decipherment of the Proto-Dravidian Indus script*. (Scandinavian Institute of Asian Studies, Special publications, no. 2.) Copenhagen.

Parpola, Asko, et al. 1970. *Further progress in the Indus script decipherment*. (Scandinavian Institute of Asian Studies, Special publications, no. 3.) Copenhagen.

Parry, Milman. 1971. *The making of Homeric verse*. London: Methuen.

Pinnow, Heinz-Jürgen. 1959. *Versuch einer historischen Lautlehre der Kharia-Sprache*. Wiesbaden: Harrassowitz.

Pischel, Richard. 1957. *Comparative grammar of the Prakrit languages*. Translated by Subhadra Jha. Varanasi: Motilal Banarsidass.

Putnam, George N., and Edna M. O'Hern. 1956. *The status significance of an isolated urban dialect*. (*Language* dissertation, no. 53.) Baltimore: Linguistic Society of America.

Rajaram, S. 1972. *Tamil phonetic reader*. Mysore: Central Institute of Indian Languages.

Ramanujan, A. K. 1963. *A generative grammar of Kannada*. Dissertation, Indiana University.

Ramanujan, A. K. 1968. The structure of variation: A study in caste dialects. In *Structure and change in Indian society*, ed. Milton Singer and Bernard S. Cohn (Viking Fund publications in anthropology, no. 47), 461–74. Chicago: Aldine.

Ramaswami Aiyar, L. V. 1927. A brief account of Malayalam phonetics. *Journal of the Dept. of Letters, University of Calcutta* 14, no. 3:8–9.

Ramaswami Aiyar, L. V. 1932a. Tulu prose texts in two dialects. *Bulletin of the School of Oriental Studies, University of London* 6:897–931.

Ramaswami Aiyar, L. V. 1932b. Tulu initial affricates and sibilants. *Quarterly Journal of the Mythic Society* (Bangalore) 22:259–73.

Ramaswami Aiyar, L. V. 1935. Dravidic sandhi, II:1, Vowels and semivowels. *Quarterly Journal of the Mythic Society* (Bangalore) 26:91–112.

Ramaswami Aiyar, L. V. 1936. Materials for a sketch of Tulu phonology. *Indian Linguistics* 6:385–438.

Rao, Shikarpur Ranganath. 1982. *The decipherment of the Indus script*. Bombay: Asia Publishing House.

Renou, Louis. 1957. Introduction générale. In Jakob Wackernagel, *Altindische Grammatik,* 2d ed., vol. 1, 1–125. Göttingen: Vandenhoeck & Ruprecht.

Rhys. Davids, Thomas W. 1903. *Buddhist India*. New York: Putnam's. Reprinted, Delhi: Motilal Banarsidass, 1971.

Salomon, Richard. 1982. Review of Gupta and Ramachandran 1979. *Journal of the American Oriental Society* 102:553–55.

Sapir, Edward. 1915. *Abnormal types of speech in Nootka*. (Geological Survey of Canada, Memoir 62, Anthropological series, no. 5.) Ottawa.

Schatzman, Leonard, and Anselm Strauss. 1955. Social class and modes of communication. *American Journal of Sociology* 60:3–29.

Schogt, Henry G. 1961. La notion de loi dans la phonétique historique. *Lingua* 10:79–92.

Sethu Pillai, R. P. 1938–39. Tamil—Literary and colloquial. *Annals of Oriental Research of the University of Madras* 2:2, 3:1, 3:2.

Shankar Bhat, D. N. 1967. *Descriptive analysis of Tulu*. (Building Centenary and Silver Jubilee series, no. 15.) Poona: Deccan College.

Shankar Bhat, D. N. 1968a. The Belari language. *Linguistic Survey Bulletin, Deccan College* 2:1–6.

Shankar Bhat, D. N. 1968b. The Tamil dialects of South Kanara. *Linguistic Survey Bulletin, Deccan College* 3:12–18.

Shankar Bhat, D. N. 1968c. The Onti dialect of Koraga, I–II. *Linguistic Survey Bulletin, Deccan College* 7:9–18, 8:5–14.

Shankar Bhat, D. N. 1968d. Review of Manappa Nayak 1967. *Linguistic Survey Bulletin, Deccan College* 8:21–26.

Shankar Bhat, D. N. 1968e. The Tappu dialect of Koraga. *Linguistic Survey Bulletin, Deccan College* 9:3–15.

Shankar Bhat, D. N. 1968f. The Mudu dialect of Koraga. *Linguistic Survey Bulletin, Deccan College* 10:9–17.

Shanmugam Pillai, M. 1956. Phonemic variation of kuṟṟiyal-ukaram in Tamil. *Indian Linguistics* 15:31–38.

Shanmugam Pillai, M. 1960. Tamil—Literary and colloquial. In Ferguson and Gumperz 1960, 27–42.

Shanmugam Pillai, M. 1962. A Tamil dialect in Ceylon. *Indian Linguistics* 23:90–98.

Shanmugam Pillai, M. 1965a. Caste isoglosses in kinship terms. *Anthropological Linguistics* 7, no. 3:59–66.

Shanmugam Pillai, M. 1965b. Merger of colloquial and literary Tamil. *Anthropological Linguistics* 7, no. 4:98–103.

Shapiro, Michael C., and Harold Schiffman (eds.) 1981. *Language and society in South Asia.* Delhi: Motilal Banarsidass.

Sharma, Aryendra. 1958. *A basic grammar of modern Hindi.* Delhi: Ministry of Education.

Sherzer, Joel. 1982. The interplay of structure and function in Kuna narrative. In Tannen 1982a, 306–22.

Sircar, Dines Chandra. 1965. *Indian epigraphy.* Delhi: Motilal Banarsidass.

Southworth, Franklin C. 1975. Cereals in South Asian prehistory: The linguistic evidence. In *Ecological backgrounds of South Asian prehistory,* ed. Kenneth A. R. Kennedy and Gregory L. Possehl (South Asia occasional papers and theses, no. 4), 52–75. Ithaca, N.Y.: South Asia Program, Cornell University.

Southworth, Franklin C. 1978. Lexical evidence for early contacts between Indo-Aryan and Dravidian. In *Aryan and non-Aryan in India,* ed. Madhav M. Deshpande and Peter E. Hook, 191–234. Ann Arbor: Center for South and Southeast Asian Studies, University of Michigan.

Spencer, Harold. 1950. *A Kanarese grammar,* revised by W. Preston. Mysore: Wesley Press.

Sreedhar, M. V. 1972. Phonology of the Cochin dialect of Malayalam. *International Journal of Dravidian Linguistics* 1:2.100–125.

Sreekantaiya, T. N. 1939. The mutation of *i, u, e* and *o* in Kannada. In *Proceedings and Transactions of the 8th All-India Oriental Congress, Mysore,* 769–800. Mysore: Maharaja's College.

Sreekantaiya, T. N. 1940. English as the Kannaḍiga speaks it. *Mysore University Bulletin of Phonetic Studies* 1:11–19.

Srinivasavarma, G. 1969. Phonology of Yerukula. In *Dravidian linguistics: Proceedings of the Seminar on Comparative Dravidian, 1968,* ed. S. Agesthialingom and N. Kumaraswami Raja, 187–202. Annamalainagar: Annamalai University.

Subrahmanya Sastri, P. S. 1930. *Tolkāppiyam: The earliest extant Tamil grammar, with a short commentary in English.* Vol. 1, *Eḻuttatikāram.* (Madras Oriental series, no. 3.) Madras: Journal of Oriental Research.

Subramoniam, V. I. 1958. *A descriptive analysis of a dialect of Tamil.* Dissertation, Indiana University.

Subramoniam, V. I. 1962. Phonemic outline of a dialect of Malayalam. *Indian Linguistics* 23:99–116.

Subramoniam, V. I. 1973. Discussion of Bright 1972a. *International Journal of Dravidian Linguistics* 2:53–55.

Syamala Kumari, B. 1972. *Malayalam phonetic reader.* Mysore: Central Institute of Indian Languages.

Tannen, Deborah (ed.) 1982a. *Analyzing discourse: Text and talk.* (Georgetown University Round Table on Languages and Linguistics, 1981.) Washington, D.C.: Georgetown University Press.

Tannen, Deborah (ed.) 1982b. *Spoken and written language: Exploring orality and literacy.* Norwood, N.J.: Ablex.

Thomason, Sarah Grey, and Terrence Kaufman. 1988. *Language contact, creolization, and genetic linguistics.* Berkeley: University of California Press.

Tiwari, Uday Narayan. 1960. *The origin and development of Bhojpuri.* (Asiatic Society monograph series, no. 10.) Calcutta.

Upadhyaya, Suseela P. 1969. *Mapila Malayalam: A descriptive and comparative study.* Dissertation, University of Poona.

Upadhyaya, U. P. 1968. *A comparative study of four Kannada dialects.* Doctoral thesis, Deccan College, Poona.

Upadhyaya, U. P. 1969. Effects of bilingualism on Bidar Kannada. *Linguistic Survey Bulletin, Deccan College* 16:1–20.

Upadhyaya, U. P. 1972. Kuruba—A Dravidian language. In *Third Seminar on Dravidian Linguistics,* ed. S. Agesthialingom and S. V. Shanmugam (Department of Linguistics, publication no. 27), 307–28. Annamalainagar: Annamalai University.

Upasak, C. S. 1960. *The history and palaeography of Mauryan Brahmi script.* Nalanda: [The author.]

Vaillant, George C. 1950. *The Aztecs of Mexico.* Harmondsworth: Penguin.

Velayudhan, S. 1973. Discussion of Bright 1972a. *International Journal of Dravidian Linguistics* 2:250–53.

Venugopala Panikkar, T. B. 1973. Discussion of Bright 1972a. *International Journal of Dravidian Linguistics* 2:50.

Verma, Thakur Prasad. 1971. *The palaeography of Brahmi script in North India, from c. 236 BC to c. 200 AD.* Varanasi: Siddharth Prakashan.

Verma, Thakur Prasad. 1979. Comment. In Gupta and Ramachandran 1979, 98–110.

Vinson, Julien. 1895. Les variations phonétiques de la prononciation populaire tamoule. *Centenaire de l'École des Langues Orientales Vivantes,* 115–26. Paris.

Voegelin, C. F. 1962. The generative criterion for deciding alternatives in descriptive linguistics. *Studies in Linguistics* 16:42–48.

Voegelin, C. F., and F. M. Voegelin. 1961. Typological classification of systems with included, excluded, and self-sufficient alphabets. *Anthropological Linguistics* 3, no. 1:55–96.

Wakankar, L. S. 1983. Writing in India—Ignorance and reality. *CALTIS 83* (Souvenir from Seminar on Calligraphy, Lettering, and Typography of Indic Scripts.) Pune: Institute of Typographical Research.

Weinreich, Uriel. 1954. Is a structural dialectology possible? *Word* 10:388–400.

Whitney, William Dwight. 1889. *Sanskrit grammar.* 2d ed. Cambridge, Mass.: Harvard University Press.

Zengel, Marjorie S. 1962. Literacy as a factor in language change. *American Anthropologist* 64:132–39.

Zide, Arlene, and Kamil Zvelebil. 1970. Review of Knorozov et al. *Language* 46:952–68.

Zurbuchen, Mary S. 1981. *The shadow theater of Bali: Explorations in language and text.* Dissertation, University of Michigan. (Published as *The language of Balinese shadow theater.* Princeton, N.J.: Princeton University Press.)

Zvelebil, Kamil. 1959. Dialects of Tamil, I–II. *Archiv Orientální* 27:272–17, 572–603.

Zvelebil, Kamil. 1960a. Dialects of Tamil, III: Madurai. *Archiv Orientální* 28:414–56.

Zvelebil, Kamil. 1960b. Notes on two dialects of Ceylon Tamil. In *Transactions of the Linguistic Circle of Delhi, Dr. Siddheswar Varma volume,* 28–36. Delhi: Linguistic Circle of Delhi.

Zvelebil, Kamil. 1961. Some features of Dindigul Tamil. In *Te. Po. Mī. Maṇiviṟā Malar (T. P. Meeenakshisundaram Commemoration volume)*, 424–46. Coimbatore: Kalaikathir Achchagam.

Zvelebil, Kamil. 1963a. On finite verb terminations in colloquial Tamil. *Archiv Orientální* 31:109–18.

Zvelebil, Kamil. 1963b. The vowels of colloquial Tamil. *Archiv Orientální* 31:225–29.

Zvelebil, Kamil. 1963c. Dialects of Tamil, IV: Erode, Tuticorin, Ramnad. *Archiv Orientální* 31:635–68.

Zvelebil, Kamil. 1970. *Comparative Dravidian phonology.* (Janua linguarum, series practica, no. 80.) The Hague: Mouton.

Index

Ingram Content Group UK Ltd.
Milton Keynes UK
UKHW010223150623
423483UK00002B/39

9 780195 063653